Illustrator®CS2
KillerTips

ILLUSTRATOR® CS2 KILLER TIPS

The Illustrator® CS2
Killer Tips Team

TECHNICAL EDITORS
Cindy Snyder
Kim Doty

PRODUCTION EDITOR
Kim Gabriel

PRODUCTION MANAGER
Dave Damstra

COVER DESIGN AND
CREATIVE CONCEPTS
Felix Nelson

PUBLISHED BY
New Riders

Copyright © 2006 by Kelby Corporate Management, Inc.

FIRST EDITION: October 2005

Composed in Myriad Pro and Helvetica by NAPP Publishing.

Trademarks
All terms mentioned in this book that are known to be trademarks or service marks have been appropriately capitalized. New Riders cannot attest to the accuracy of this information. Use of a term in the book should not be regarded as affecting the validity of any trademark or service mark.

Illustrator is a registered trademark of Adobe Systems, Inc.
Windows is a registered trademark of Microsoft Corporation.

Warning and Disclaimer
This book is designed to provide information about Illustrator tips. Every effort has been made to make this book as complete and as accurate as possible, but no warranty of fitness is implied.

The information is provided on an as-is basis. The authors and New Riders shall have neither liability nor responsibility to any person or entity with respect to any loss or damages arising from the information contained in this book or from the use of the discs or programs that may accompany it.

ISBN 0-321-33065-X

9 8 7 6 5 4 3 2

Printed and bound in the United States of America

www.peachpit.com
www.scottkelbybooks.com

To the most important people in my life: my Mom and Dad, my sisters Julie and Deb, and my family: Marlene, Stephanie, and Michael.

—Dave Cross

To those that I have trained over the years—thank you for making this all worth it and allowing me to do what I love to do.

—Matt Kloskowski

ACKNOWLEDGMENTS

There are many, many advantages to having a co-author on a book like this one, and one pretty big drawback. I think the advantages are pretty obvious: the whole two-heads-are-better-than-one thing. It has been a great pleasure to work with Matt on this book—and on the many other things we work on together on a day-to-day basis. So, what's the downside? I only have half a page for my acknowledgments, whereas last time I had a full page. Oh well…

If you've read any books that are produced at KW Media, you've probably read the author going on and on about how great the team is at KW, but it really is true! I can't imagine being able to produce high-quality books like this one without our great team (I know I certainly wouldn't want to try). You people are all CRAZY—and I love you for it. Thanks to Kim Gabriel for her unbelievable scheduling/balancing act routine, to Felix Nelson for always tweaking our designs to make them better, to our newest Technical Editors Cindy Snyder and Kim Doty for jumping right into the fire and making sure everything worked, and to Dave Damstra for once again making things fit and look pretty. My continuing gratitude to Scott Kelby, Kalebra Kelby, and Jean Kendra for convincing me to move to Florida, and for making this such a cool place to work. Mr. Moser, what can I say but thank you sir, again (as you were).

Thanks to the artists who very generously provided artwork for us to use in the book. It is much better as a result of their stunning Illustrator work.

Finally, I need to acknowledge my family for their love and support. As I write this, it's my 21st wedding anniversary and my 18-year-old daughter is about to head off to college. It's hard to believe that it's been that long, since every day is like a honeymoon (a honeymoon with two grown kids, I guess). Marlene, you are the love of my life and I look forward to every minute we spend together. Stephanie and Michael, there may be fathers who are prouder of their kids than I am, but I find that hard to believe. You make me smile just thinkin' about ya. (Yes Cassy, you too). All-in-all, I consider myself one darn lucky guy.

—*DAVE CROSS*

First, I'd like to thank my co-author and boss, Dave Cross, for involving me with this book. Not only is he an all-around great guy but he's a constant reminder to me of a 100% "class act" in this business. It's an honor to work with him. I'd also like to thank my co-workers and friends at KW Media Group who, in a short time, have shown me how they continually push the boundaries of quality and excellence in every aspect of this business.

I'd also like to thank the illustrators who have allowed us to use their work in this book and the folks at Adobe, namely Julieanne Kost and Terry White, for quickly getting us up to speed on the latest version of Illustrator. Special thanks go out to the folks at Peachpit Press, as well, for helping me do what I love, which is to train and educate people.

Next, I'd like to thank my family. My mom, dad, brother, and sister have always been a great source of inspiration and support to me. Without you, I'd never have gotten such a great start to such a wonderful life.

Speaking of wonderful lives, my greatest thanks goes to my wife, Diana, and two sons, Ryan and Justin, for making my life the best I could have ever dreamed of. The three of you are the reason I wake up every day, and I can never express my gratitude to you for making me feel like the luckiest husband/dad ever.

—*MATT KLOSKOWSKI*

ABOUT THE AUTHORS

Dave Cross

Dave Cross is Senior Developer, Education and Curriculum, for the National Association of Photoshop Professionals and is involved in all aspects of the training that is provided to NAPP members, including the content of seminars, conferences and workbooks. He also creates the very popular weekly QuickTime-based tutorials that appear on the members' website. Dave is an Adobe Certified Instructor in Photoshop CS2 and Illustrator CS2, and is a Certified Technical Trainer.

Prior to joining NAPP, Dave lived in Canada and trained thousands of users across North America. He has been using and teaching Illustrator and Photoshop since their original versions, starting in 1987. Dave co-authored the *Photoshop World Dream Team Book, Volume One*, and is the author of *The Photoshop CS2 Help Desk Book*. Dave writes the "Classic Photoshop Effects" and "Beginners' Workshop" columns for *Photoshop User* magazine, teaches at the Photoshop World Conference & Expo, and is the Lead Instructor for the Photoshop Seminar Tour. He also is featured on a series of DVDs, such as *Best of Photoshop User, Photoshop CS2 for Beginners*, and *Photoshop CS2 Layer Techniques*.

In his spare time, Dave is the Graphics Editor for *Layers* magazine, and enjoys freaking out his Florida co-workers by wearing shorts to work every day, simply "because he can." Dave lives in Odessa, Florida, with his wife, Marlene, and children, Stephanie and Michael.

Matt Kloskowski

Matt Kloskowski is the Education and Curriculum Developer for the National Association of Photoshop Professionals, where he eats, sleeps, and breathes Photoshop and Adobe training to NAPP members. Matt has written four books on Photoshop and Illustrator, including *Photoshop CS2 Savvy, Extreme Photoshop CS*, and *Illustrator CS Most Wanted*. He's featured on various training DVDs available from www.photoshopvideos.com, and is a regular contributing writer to *Photoshop User* magazine, *Layers* magazine, and the *Photoshop Elements Techniques* newsletter. Matt is an instructor at Photoshop World and the Mac Design Conference, and is an Adobe Certified Expert in Photoshop, as well as a Macromedia Flash Certified Developer. He teaches basic and advanced Photoshop classes for Sessions Online School of Design (www.sessions.edu).

TABLE OF CONTENTS

TABLE OF CONTENTS

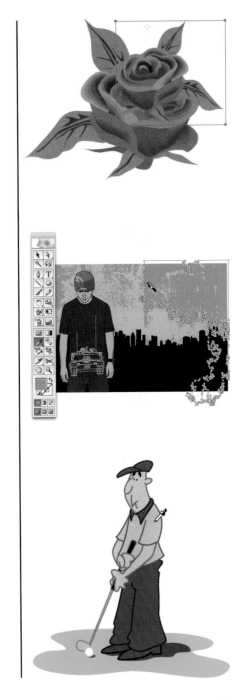

TABLE OF CONTENTS

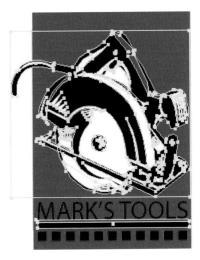

TABLE OF CONTENTS

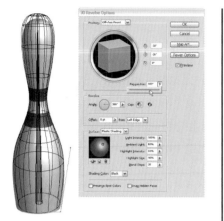

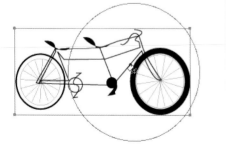

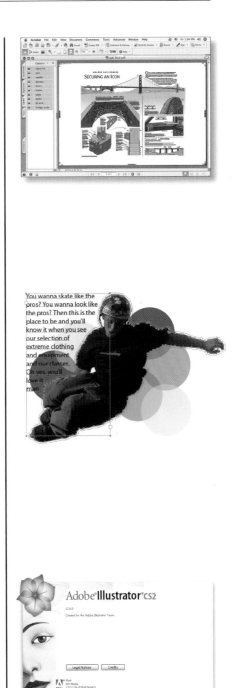

TABLE OF CONTENTS

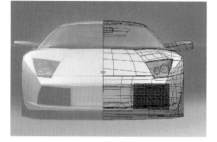

INTRODUCTION

The idea behind this book

The very first *Killer Tips* book was created based on the premise that the first thing everyone reads in any book is the sidebars. You know, the quick little tips that are typically accompanied by some icon to emphasize their importance. We're no different: We get a new book and flip through it, looking for the tips and then (maybe) will get around to reading the actual text in the chapter. This book is a blatant attempt to capitalize on the popularity of the *Photoshop Killer Tips* book by making up a bunch of stuff and slapping a cover onto it that implies it might actually be useful. Of course we're kidding here—only a handful of the tips were made up; the majority of the others work fine (the ones we tested anyway).

This *Killer Tips* book is a little different from the others in the series, as we revisited the question, "What makes a tip a killer tip?" and realized that it really depends on your experience with the software. To a beginner, a "killer" tip could be a simple shortcut that the more experienced Illustrator user has known for years. So, we created a "Basic Training" chapter with a whole series of what amount to "Killer Tips for Beginners." But throughout the pages, the underlying theme is the same as all the *Killer Tips* books—speed. Get it done fast and do it accurately (and enjoy the new speed at which you can create your works of art).

Is this book for you?

Yes. There, that was simple wasn't it? Yes, you should buy this book. Read it if you must, but definitely buy it. No, really, this book is aimed at the two main types of Illustrator users out there. There's the everyday Illustrator users who have been creating all kinds of cool designs but just want to be faster. They crave speed and quicker ways to get their artwork done. These users will find all kinds of productivity tips and important reminders of speedier methods and helpful techniques. Then there's the other kind of Illustrator user: the ones who own the software and use it occasionally or are just getting started. They will enjoy the fact that some of the tips cover the important principles of the program, particularly the ones that aren't self-evident.

Of course, one of the biggest challenges in a book like this is to decide which tips are "too" basic, which tips "everyone knows," and which tips are way beyond comprehension except for rocket scientists. Our simple solution was to throw darts at a dartboard filled with tip-laden sticky notes, and hope that all the best tips didn't get left out. We believe the odds were in our favor. Seriously, our goal was to provide a wide range of tips, so if the first couple cause you to say, "Jeez, I knew that!" that's great! That means you've done a good job of teaching yourself about Illustrator. Keep on truckin', though, and we know you'll find tips that will change your life (or at least make things go a lot faster).

Is this book for Mac or Windows, or both?

This book is for anyone that owns Illustrator: any platform, any version. Yes, if you run Illustrator 88 on your Mac SE, you can benefit from the seven tips that relate to your version. Of course, if you are using Illustrator CS2 on OS X or Windows, then all of these tips will be of interest to you. For each tip that includes a keyboard command, we give you both the Macintosh and Windows version of the shortcut. Sorry, but due to space constraints we had to cut the Amiga keyboard shortcuts from each tip. Maybe next time.

How to use this book

The beauty of a book like this lies in its simplicity: Start reading anywhere, stop reading when you're finished. Remember, the first chapter is really aimed more at inexperienced users (but it's okay for you to read that one too, even if you feel pretty comfortable with Illustrator—you never know what you might have missed).

If you really want to take best advantage of this book, we would recommend using it with at least three of the following: candlelight, hot tub, wine, favorite companion, barbershop quartet music. Can you imagine anything more romantic? Reading aloud some Illustrator tips by candle-light to your loved one, to the *a capella* strains of "Heart of My Heart"…

ANOTHER TIP

You're doing it again! Stop looking at these sidebars. See, they're intoxi-cating—you're drawn to them even after you know it's not really a tip. Okay, here's a real tip: If you like sidebar tips, buy this book.

Basic Training

BASIC TIPS
YOU CAN'T
LIVE WITHOUT

Let's start at the very beginning, that's a good place to start. Do re mi, do re mi...

Who'd-a thunk that Maria was an Illustrator user?

Basic Training!
basic tips you can't live without

Okay, so this chapter has little or nothing to do with The Sound of Music, *although it could be argued that these tips will be music to your ears when you realize how productive they'll make you. (Ha! They said it couldn't be done, but we were sure it would somehow be possible to work a classic movie musical into a chapter intro.) Before you have any second thoughts about returning the book to its place of purchase, let us reassure you that these introductions are in no way a reflection of the practical and useful tips that follow them. Go ahead, breathe that big sigh of relief.*

MAKE YOURSELF FAMOUS

OK, so it's a stretch to include this tip anywhere, but I thought it was cool. Make yourself famous by appearing in the Credits that display on a PC when you choose Help>About Illustrator and click on the Credits button. Just modify the file located in Adobe Illustrator CS2\Support Files\Contents\Windows. The file name is CreditsText.utxt and it opens in any basic text editor. Add your name into it, save it, and show the credits. You can impress all of your friends by saying you were on the product team. (Okay, maybe that's exaggerating a bit. They probably won't believe you, but it's still fun.)

ADDITIONAL CONTENT

If you haven't realized this yet, Illustrator CS2 comes with a ton of extra content. This includes fonts, symbols, swatches, gradients, styles, and custom brushes. I can't stress this one enough. If you need some creative inspiration, then check out this content. It's located right inside the Presets folder (in the Adobe Illustrator Applications or Program File on your hard drive) and is categorized based on what type of preset it works with (i.e., brushes, patterns, gradients, symbols, etc.).

MORE ADDITIONAL CONTENT

If you liked the previous tip, but thought to yourself, "How am I supposed to ever see all of this content so I can choose what I like?" then I've got some good news and some bad news for you. Which do you want first? I always take the good news first, so that's where we'll start. Illustrator CS included a PDF file called Additional Content.pdf that showed a high resolution preview of all the presets. The bad news is that Illustrator CS2 doesn't, so it's basically a guessing game. If you have Illustrator CS, then the PDF file is located in Illustrator CS\ Additional Content.pdf.

WACOM PEN TABLETS WORK IN ILLUSTRATOR TOO

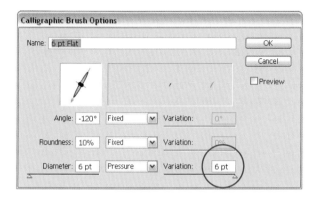

Many people don't know that Wacom pen tablets work great in Illustrator. It mimics traditional drawing techniques because you actually hold a Wacom pen just like you would a drawing pen or pencil. Also, the pressure-sensitive nature of the Wacom pen allows you to control the width of brush strokes in Illustrator. Try it out. Grab the pen and tablet and double-click on any Calligraphic Brush in the Brushes palette (under the Window menu) to bring up the Calligraphic Brush Options dialog. Under one of the settings, such as Diameter, select Pressure, make the variation setting higher, and click OK. Then try drawing on the artboard. Press down softer and harder with the pen and you'll see that the strokes do indeed reflect how hard you are pressing.

Pressing lightly with the Wacom pen *Pressing harder with the Wacom pen* *Pressing very hard with the Wacom pen*

 **ONGOING FEEDBACK**

If you're ever unsure that you're holding down the correct modifier key, check out the Status Bar in the lower left hand corner: It constantly changes based on what you're doing. For example, if you have the Rectangle tool (M) active it will display "Rectangle." Press-and-hold the Command key (PC: Control key) and start to drag the object and it will display "Move." Throw in Option-Shift (PC: Alt-Shift) while dragging, and the display will change to "Constrain and Copy." It's a simple but effective way to reassure yourself that you're using the correct keys. *Note:* If you do not see the tool name, click on the Status Bar and under Show, choose Current Tool.

TIMING IS EVERYTHING

One of the more important principles of using keyboard modifiers is that the same key will have different effects, depending on when you use it. For example, with the Direct Selection tool (A) active, holding down the Option key (PC: Alt key) will select the entire path. If you don't let go of the Option key when you drag, you'll get a copy. So in this case, to move a path without copying it, press-and-hold the Option key and click on the path, then let go of the Option key before dragging the path.

 THE EVER-CHANGING PALETTE

Many Illustrator palettes have more than one display size—in some cases, multiple sizes. You can use a palette's flyout menu to choose Show Options or Hide Options, but it can be faster to double-click on the tab at the top of the palette. To see if a palette has multiple sizes, just keep double-clicking on the tab to switch among the collapsed, basic, and expanded views. (Why collapse palettes? To save space without closing palettes or to move them out of the way.)

Collapsed palette

Basic size

Expanded palette

 QUICK DELETE FROM PALETTES

To delete anything from a palette, without getting a dialog like this example asking you to confirm your choice, hold down the Option key (PC: Alt key) as you click on the palette's Trash icon. This applies to brushes, swatches, layers, etc.

 **LOCKING AND UNLOCKING GUIDES**

By default, all guides that you add to a document are locked. To unlock all the guides in one quick step, press Command-Option-; (PC: Control-Alt-;). This also works the other way around: Once you've unlocked all the guides, use the same shortcut to lock all guides.

CHOOSE THE BEST SELECTION TOOL FOR THE JOB

Trying to determine when to use the Selection tool (V) versus the Direct Selection tool (A)? Here's a simple suggestion: Think of the Selection tool as the "move" tool and the Direct Selection tool as the "reshaping" tool. Actually, I suppose that the Selection tool should be thought of as the move/resize tool, since those are the two functions it performs. So, anytime you need to decide between tools, ask yourself, "Do I need to move/resize the object or reshape it?" That will help you pick the correct selection tool.

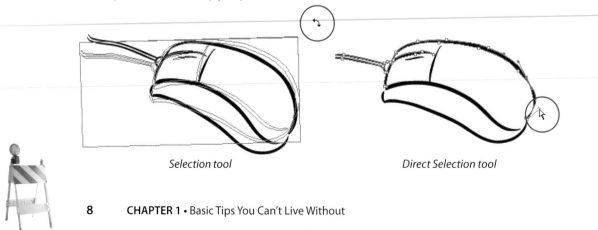

Selection tool   *Direct Selection tool*

DIRECT SELECTION SECRET

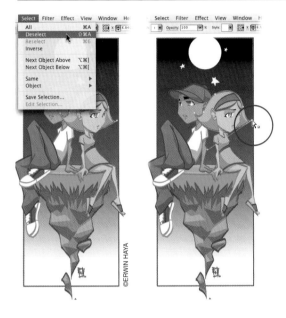

©ERWIN HAYA

If you're having trouble getting the Direct Selection tool (A) to select only one individual point, here are two "secrets" to success. (1) Make sure nothing is selected by either clicking away from any object or by pressing Command-Shift-A (PC: Control-Shift-A). (2) If you click on the fill of an object, the Direct Selection tool will act just like the Selection tool. So, make sure no anchor points are selected, and then position your mouse over one anchor point and click.

QUICK SELECTION TOOL

If you need to use the Selection tool (V) and then return to the tool you were using, here's how to do it. With any tool selected, press-and-hold the Command key (PC: Control key) to temporarily activate the Selection tool. (Actually, it will activate the last selection tool you used, so you may get the Direct Selection tool.) Once you've used the Selection tool, let go of the key to return to whatever tool you had been using.

HIDE BOUNDING BOX

Here's a shortcut that you'll want to memorize—the ability to show and hide the bounding box. The bounding box is a great way to resize objects without switching to the Scale tool (S). On the other hand, sometimes the bounding box is very distracting, so the option to show or hide it is very useful. Just press Command-Shift-B (PC: Control-Shift-B) each time you want to toggle the bounding box on and off.

QUICK MOVE DIALOG

A quick way to access the Move dialog is to double-click on the Selection tool. That saves you from having to dig down in the Object menu to get to the command.

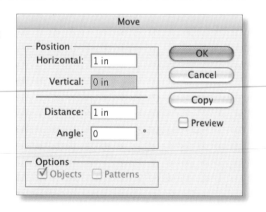

SELECTING THE NEXT OBJECT BELOW

If you know there's an object hidden under another object and you need to select it, use the contextual menu. With the Selection tool (V), click on the top object, then Control-click (PC: Right-click) and from the contextual menu choose Select>Next Object Below (as we did here to select the airplane). You'll notice there are similar commands for objects above.

CREATE BY MEASURE

You can create an object at a specific size by choosing the appropriate shape tool (Rectangle, Star, etc.) and then clicking on the artboard. In the subsequent dialog, enter the exact measurements you'd like to use and click OK. To create a shape that's centered on the position of your click, hold down the Option key (PC: Alt key) when you click on the artboard. *Bonus:* Want to know the size of the shape you just created by dragging? Click once using that shape's tool and check out the numbers in the dialog (then click Cancel).

POSITION SHAPES AS YOU DRAW

With any of the shape tools, you can change the position of the shape while you create it on the artboard. Simply hold down the Spacebar to "interrupt" the tool you're using, allowing you to move the shape. Let go of the Spacebar to continue drawing the shape.

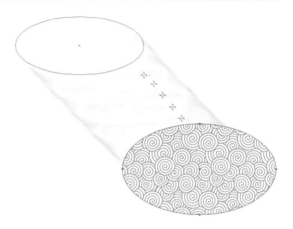

DRAWING CURVES MORE EASILY

If you're new to drawing curves with the Pen tool (P), here's a quick method to create a simple curve. Use the Pen tool to draw two straight lines that create a triangle that points in the direction you want your curve. Then hold down the Option key (PC: Alt key) to activate the Convert Anchor Point tool. Click on the anchor point where the two lines meet and drag outwards to create a curve.

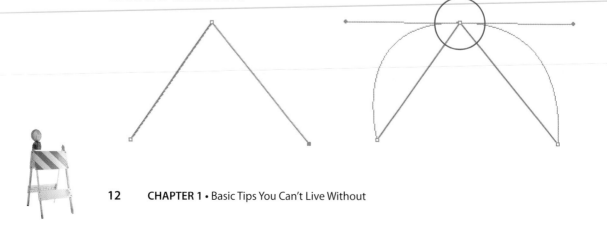

SIMPLIFYING A PATH

One of the basic rules of Illustrator should be to use the minimum number of anchor points that you can get away with on a path. This will keep your objects as simple as possible, which will help streamline the printing process. An easy way to reduce the number of anchor points on a path is to select the path and use the Simplify command (Object>Path>Simplify).

SELECT NONE

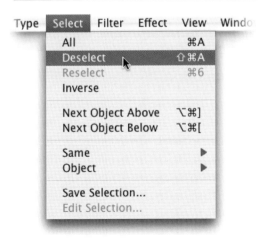

Hopefully, you know that the command to select everything (Select All) is Command-A (PC: Control-A). That's pretty standard in most programs. In Illustrator, it's just as easy to ensure that nothing is selected. To do this, press Command-Shift-A (PC: Control-Shift-A). Or, if you want to do it the "old-fashioned way," go to the Select menu and choose Deselect (as shown here).

EVERYTHING ELSE BUT

To select everything except one object, select the object, then from the Select menu choose Inverse.

 WHAT HAPPENS WHEN YOU CAN'T SEE AN OBJECT?

If you have objects that have no stroke or fill, they are—in effect—hidden. To select one of these paths, look for a small square to appear beside the Selection tool (V). This tells you that you are directly over a path. You can also click-and-drag in the general area of the object using one of the selection tools to select the path.

EVEN IT OUT

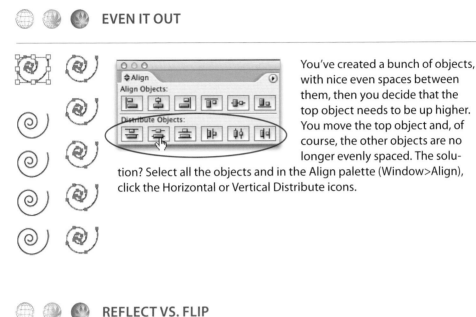

You've created a bunch of objects, with nice even spaces between them, then you decide that the top object needs to be up higher. You move the top object and, of course, the other objects are no longer evenly spaced. The solution? Select all the objects and in the Align palette (Window>Align), click the Horizontal or Vertical Distribute icons.

REFLECT VS. FLIP

In almost every application, there are commands called Flip Vertical and Flip Horizontal—in Illustrator they're not so obvious. There's the Reflect tool (O), but that's more like a mirror reflection than a flip. In other words, Reflect Horizontal is the equivalent of Flip Vertical. That's because "horizontal" indicates the angle of your mirror, which—in effect—flips your object vertically. In case you find that too confusing, commands for Flip Horizontal and Flip Vertical are found in the flyout menu in the Transform palette (Window>Transform).

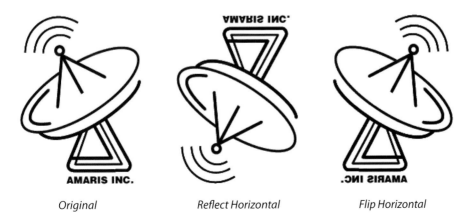

Original   *Reflect Horizontal*   *Flip Horizontal*

CHAPTER 1 • Basic Tips You Can't Live Without   **15**

 **TOOL PREFERENCES**

A number of tools have individual preferences or options that you can change to affect the way the tool performs. To open a tool's preferences or options, double-click any of these tools in the Toolbox: Line, Arc, Rectangular Grid, Polar Grid, Flare, Paintbrush, Pencil, Smooth, Eyedropper, Blend, Paint Bucket, Paint Selection, Measure, and any Liquify, Symbolism, or Graph tools.

Paintbrush Tool Preferences	
Tolerances	
Fidelity: 4 pixels	OK
Smoothness: 0 percent	Cancel
	Reset
Options	
☐ Fill new brush strokes	
☑ Keep Selected	
☑ Edit Selected Paths	
Within: 12 pixels	

 **NAME A SWATCH**

After creating a new swatch, you can always name it after the fact by double-clicking on it. Or you can name a new swatch as you create it by pressing the Option key (PC: Alt key) as you click on the New Swatch icon at the bottom of the Swatches palette (Window>Swatches).

New Swatch	
Swatch Name: dark brown	OK
Color Type: Process Color	Cancel
☐ Global	
Color Mode: CMYK	
C 23 %	
M 55 %	
Y 94.12 %	
K 38 %	

RESET THE DEFAULT FILL AND STROKE COLORS

To get back to the default colors of a white fill and black stroke, press D (for default). Needless to say, this shortcut doesn't work if you're using the Type tool.

Default Fill and Stroke (D)

COLOR PICKER

To access a Photoshop-style Color Picker, double-click on either the Fill or Stroke icon near the bottom of the Tool-box or in the top-left of the Color palette. Choose a color visually or numerically, click OK, and you're done.

HIDE OR SHOW MULTIPLE LAYERS EASILY

If you have a long list of layers or sublayers and need to hide a bunch of them—but not all of them—click-and-drag through the Eye icons in the Layers palette to hide or show the layers. Of course, this only works with contiguous layers, but it sure works well, and fast.

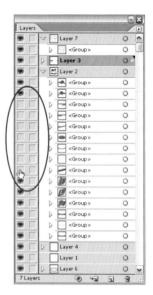

FILTERS VS. EFFECTS?

What's the main difference between the two? Effects are more flexible, allowing you to edit the effect through the Appearance palette (Window>Appearance), but they require more memory and processor power. Filters are "permanent" (although you can choose Undo from the Edit menu), but typically they don't take as long to process. In our example, we first applied the Roughen filter (Filter>Distort>Roughen), and then we applied the Roughen effect (Effect>Distort & Transform>Roughen), which is editable in the Appearance palette.

Filter   *Effect*

EDIT EXISTING PATTERNS AND SYMBOLS

If you see a pattern in the Swatches palette (Window>Swatches) or symbol in the Symbols palette (Window>Symbols) that you'd like to adapt by changing colors or by adding or deleting objects, drag the swatch or symbol onto the artboard. Patterns are editable, but with symbols you'll have to choose Object>Expand to be able to edit the original artwork. Once you've made your changes (using the Direct Selection tool, most likely), select the objects and drag them back into their appropriate palettes, which creates a new pattern or symbol.

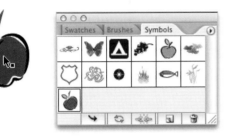

USE TEXT IMPORT OPTIONS

You can make your life a little easier when you place text by setting the options in the importing options dialog that appears before the text is placed. Depending on the type of text file, you'll get a different dialog upon placing (File>Place). Word documents, for example, offer a few choices, such as including a table of contents or removing text formatting. Text files (TXT) will cause the Text Import Options dialog to open, with more options such as removing extra carriage returns or replacing extra spaces with a tab.

SCALE TEXT FRAME BUT NOT TEXT

To make a text frame bigger, so the text reflows, click with the Selection tool (V) to make the bounding box visible. Then click-and-drag on a handle to resize the text frame without affecting the size of the type. In contrast, if you select a text frame with the Selection tool, and then use the Scale tool (S) or Free Transform tool (E), any adjustments to the text frame will scale the size of the text inside the frame.

Scaling text frame with Selection tool

Scaling text frame and text with Free Transform tool

MULTIPLE GLYPH CHOICES

Take a look in the Glyphs palette (Window>Type>Glyphs), and if an OpenType font is selected in the pop-up menu at the bottom of the palette, you will see a small black triangle at the bottom right of some of the characters. The triangle indicates that there is more than one choice for that character. Click-and-hold on one of these characters to see the choices, move your cursor over the character that you want, and release the mouse button to add that character to the artboard. This palette also serves as a great preview of a font—just choose a different typeface from the pop-up menu for an instant preview of the characters in that font.

Adobe Caslon Pro offers multiple choices as compared to Century Old Style

EFFECTING A STROKE OR A FILL

One of the advantages of the Appearance palette (Windows>Appearance) is the option to affect only the stroke or only the fill of a selected object. A great example of that is to apply an effect (not a filter) to only the stroke, or only to the fill. In the Appearance palette, click on the word Stroke and then apply an effect from the Effect menu. (In our example, we used the Roughen effect under Distort & Transform in the Effect menu—first applied just to the stroke, and then applied only to the fill.)

TRANSFORM AGAIN

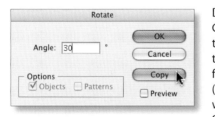

Don't be fooled by the shortcut for this command: Command-D (PC: Control-D). In many applications that's the shortcut for Duplicate, but not in Illustrator. In this program the command is called Transform Again, and it's quite different from duplicating (in a very good way). Transform Again is a shorter way of saying, "Whatever you just did, do it again." So if you just rotated an object 30°, pressing Command-D (PC: Control-D) will rotate the object another 30°. The object will not be duplicated unless that's part of the original transformation. For example, if you drag an object with the Option key (PC: Alt key) held down to move a copy, Transform Again will move another copy the exact same distance and angle. This is an extremely powerful command that has many uses! (Just remember not to do any additional operation, or you will alter your Transform Again command.)

CREATE YOUR OWN CROP MARKS

You can easily create crop marks around a graphic (to indicate where a graphic should be trimmed, for example). Just draw a rectangle that represents the crop area (don't worry about fill or stroke, they'll automatically change). With the rectangle selected, go to Object>Crop Area>Make. If you ever need to change the crop marks, use Object>Crop Area>Release and then edit the rectangle. (*Note:* The cropping object must be a non-rotated rectangle that is not being used as a clipping mask.)

OPEN A TEMPLATE

Adobe was kind enough to provide many useful templates and a simple way to make use of them, so why not take advantage of it? If you need to design artwork for a CD, for example, choose File>New From Template. You should be directed to the templates folder (Illustrator CS2\Cool Extras\Templates), where you select from the various folders. In this example, we opened the template in the Extreme Sports folder called DVD Label.ait. A new, untitled document is created that contains all the artwork, ready to edit, and the original template artwork is untouched, ready for next time.

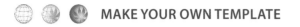

 MAKE YOUR OWN TEMPLATE

You can easily make your own template and save it in a format that will automatically be opened as an untitled copy of your artwork. Create your artwork complete with sample text, guides, and the colors you want, and then use File>Save As Template. Name the file and save it in the Templates folder for easy retrieval (it should default to AIT format, but check just to be sure). From then on, use the File>New From Template command to open your template—ready to edit—then save it as a regular Illustrator document.

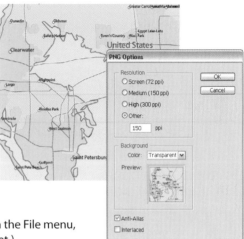

SAVE FOR MICROSOFT OFFICE

Imagine that this command under the File menu is really called "Save As a PNG File, But Without Seeing Any Options." Sure, PNG is a great format for use in MS Office, but personally, I'd like a little more control over how it's saved, such as the resolution and whether the background is transparent. To be able to see—and change—the save options, use the File>Export command instead of Save for Microsoft Office. Choose PNG in the Format (PC: Save As Type) pop-up menu, name the file, and click Export (PC: Save) to see the PNG Options dialog, where you can make changes. (Or you could select the Save for Web command in the File menu, choosing PNG in the pop-up menu under Preset.)

VIEW ACTIONS IN BUTTON MODE

In the Actions palette (found under the Window menu), you can record, edit, and play automated functions to speed up your work. In the Actions palette's standard view, every step of an action is visible and can be turned on and off. The other possible view is Button Mode (chosen from the palette's flyout menu). In Button Mode, you only see the name of the action and its keyboard shortcut, if one has been assigned. So you can use this display mode to either click on an action to play it, or to remind yourself of the F-key shortcut.

Standard view   *Button Mode view*

To return to standard view, go back to the palette's flyout menu and deselect Button Mode. (*Note:* If you've assigned a modifier key to your shortcut, such as the Shift key, this will not be reflected in the Button Mode—for some reason. You'll only see the Function key listed.)

"HIDDEN" KEYBOARD COMMANDS

In Chapter 2, we show you how to customize your own keyboard shortcuts. Here's one little extra tip that you may discover on your own, but we thought we'd make sure that you did by adding it in here. There are a few unusual commands that are kinda "hidden" in the Keyboard Shortcuts dialog (Edit>Keyboard Shortcuts). With Menu Commands selected in the top-left pop-up menu, scroll down to the very bottom of the dialog and click on the triangle beside any of the Other options (e.g., Other Select, Other Text, etc.). Look in those lists and you'll find useful keyboard commands, such as Switch Selection Tools or New Swatch.

Keyboard Shortcuts			
Set: [Custom]			
Menu Commands	Shortcut	Symbol	
▽ Other Palette			
Show Color Palette (Secondary)			
Actions Batch			
Add New Fill	Ctrl+/	/	
Add New Stroke	Alt+Ctrl+/	/	
New Graphic Style			
New Layer	Ctrl+L	L	
New Layer with Dialog	Alt+Ctrl+L	L	
Update Link			
Navigator Options			
New Swatch	*Alt+Shift+Ctrl+F5*	*F5*	
▷ Other Misc			

Buttons: OK, Cancel, Save..., Delete..., Export Text..., Undo, Clear, Go To

The View

VIEWING, DOING, UNDOING, AND MORE

Most people remember it vividly: The
first time you zoom in on a vector image
and still see sharp, clean edges. Brings a tear to

The View

viewing, doing, undoing, and more

the eye doesn't it? When you've lived in a world
dominated by Photoshop and pixels—you
know, that slightly superior, "look what I did to
this photo" attitude—it is such a rush to zoom in
to 20,000% without even a hint of jaggedness!
You know what we're talking about right?
Right? Hmmm, maybe it's just vector junkies
like us that experience that thrill? But you have
to admit, custom views and workspaces rock,
right? Right???

HOW MANY UNDOS?

Illustrator has (virtually) unlimited undos. Of course, you could keep pressing Command-Z (PC: Control-Z) over and over again until you run out of undos, but there is an easier way to know how many undos you actually have available. Click on the Status Bar at the bottom-left of the document window (next to your document size). From the pop-up menu that appears, under Show, choose Number of Undos. Now, you can see how many you've got and undo away.

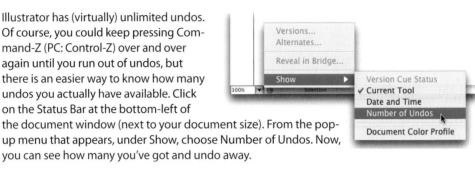

ACTUAL SIZE, FIT IN WINDOW

In Illustrator, there is often more than one way to do things, and zooming in and out is no different. You can use keyboard shortcuts to change the view to Actual Size (Command-1 [PC: Control-1]) and Fit in Window (Command-Zero [PC: Control-Zero]), and you can also change to these views using the Toolbox. Double-click on the Zoom tool to change to Actual Size view, double-click on the Hand tool to change to Fit in Window.

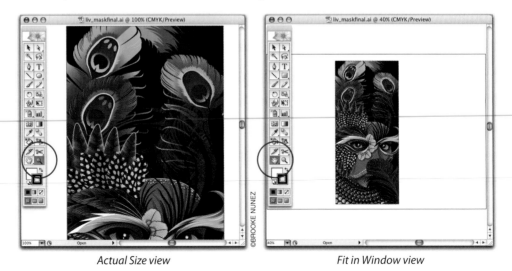

Actual Size view   *Fit in Window view*

REALLY FIT IN WINDOW

Press Command-Zero (PC: Control-Zero) to change the view to Fit in Window. If that's not zoomed out far enough, try this: Hold down the Command key (PC: Control key) and double-click on the Zoom tool in the Toolbox. The view will change to 3.13%, the smallest zoom view possible, which is ideal for those poster-size images.

©MIKE SELLERS/PENCILS BY ESTHER SLAYTON

SWITCHING BETWEEN MULTIPLE OPEN WINDOWS

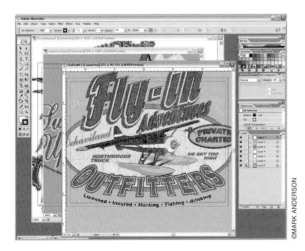

©MARK ANDERSON

Before Illustrator CS2, the only way you could switch between open windows was to go through the Window menu and choose the file you'd like to work on. Or, if you were adventurous, you could always do (our personal favorite) the window/palette shuffle and just try to maneuver your open windows around the screen. You'll be happy to know that Illustrator CS2 now has a keyboard shortcut for this: Command-~ (that's the Tilde key, right over your Tab key) on a Mac or Control-Shift-F6 on a PC.

DEFAULT WORKSPACE TO THE RESCUE!

With Illustrator CS2, we now have the ability to use workspaces. Basically, a workspace is the way that, well, the workspace is set up (i.e., palette and Toolbox locations). This is huge if you're like us and your palettes become a jumbled mess halfway through working on your images, or if you're an instructor in a classroom and find it tedious to manually reset palette locations of 20 or 30 computers after a class. To help out, just choose Window>Workspace>[Default]. This will reset the Toolbox and the palettes to their default locations.

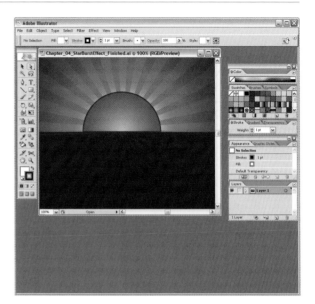

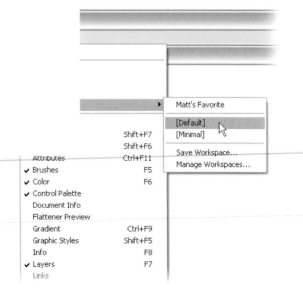

YOUR OWN PERSONAL WORKSPACE

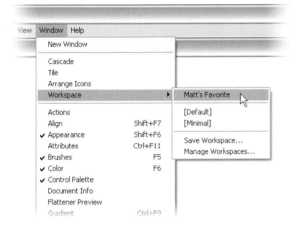

One of the most useful areas of the new Workspace feature in CS2 is the ability to create your own personal workspaces. To do this, set up the palettes you want where you want them. Then choose Window>Workspace>Save Workspace. Give it a meaningful name and you're in business. Now, if your palettes ever get to the point where everything is a mess (come on, you know it happens to you), then just go under Window>Workspace and pick your own personal workspace. It'll be right near the top of the menu.

GIVE YOUR CUSTOM WORKSPACE A SHORTCUT

Although you can save your own workspace (Window>Workspace>Save Workspace) in CS2, you cannot assign it a keyboard shortcut. Instead, record an Action: Click the Create New Action button at the bottom of the Actions palette (Window>Actions), give it a function-key shortcut and press Begin Recording. Then use the flyout menu in the Actions palette to choose Insert Menu Item and go to Window>Workspace to select your custom workspace. Press the Stop Playing/Recording button at the bottom of the Actions palette, and from now on you can press that F-key to change to your workspace.

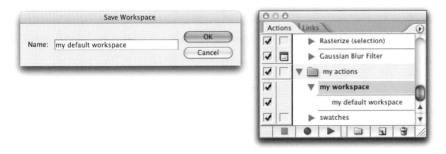

CONTROL BAR GETTING IN YOUR WAY?

The new context-sensitive Control palette in Illustrator CS2 is a great way to discover new features and find existing features faster. The ability to access selection-based tools from a single location eliminates the need for multiple palettes. However, sometimes it can be cluttered, especially if you find you don't use many of its features. If this is the case, then turn some of them off. Just click the small right-facing arrow all the way at the far right of the palette to get the flyout menu. Then click on any items you don't want it to display anymore.

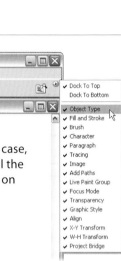

PALETTE SHORTCUTS AND CONTROL PALETTE ALL IN ONE

If you use the new Control Palette often, but still have the need to use some of the extended settings that normally appear in a specific palette, then just click on any of the setting names that are underlined and highlighted in blue. For example, the Control Palette displays Opacity, but no Blend Mode settings that you'd normally find in the Transparency palette. Instead of moving to the Transparency palette, just click on the word Opacity and a small palette will pop up below it allowing you to change more than just Opacity.

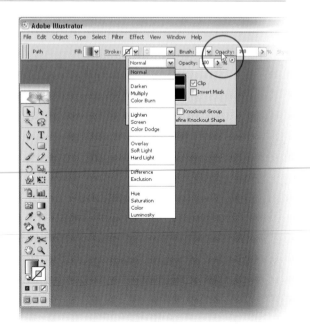

CENTER THAT GUIDE

If you drag a guide from the ruler onto the page and you want to make sure it is centered horizontally or vertically, try this: Press Command-Option-; (PC: Control-Alt-;) to unlock the guides. If necessary, make sure that only the one guide is selected by deselecting every guide and then clicking on the guide you want centered. Then in the Align palette (Window>Align), use the flyout menu to select Align to Artboard. Click on the Vertical Align Center icon (or Horizontal Align Center icon, depending on the direction of the guide).

CENTER GUIDES AUTOMATICALLY

You may be thinking, why not record an action to add centered guides automatically? (I know I was.) You can, but with a bit of a trick. Problem is, you cannot record adding a guide to the page, so you have to use another method. Use the Pen tool (P) (with the Shift key held down) to draw a horizontal line that is wider than the current page, and keep the line selected. In the Actions palette under the Window menu, click the Create New Action icon, give your action a name, and press Begin Recording. Then use the Action palette's flyout menu and choose Insert Select Path. Next, click on the Vertical Align Center icon in the Align palette (be sure the Align to Artboard option is selected in the palette's flyout menu), followed by View>Guides>Make Guides. Click the Stop Playing/Recording icon in the Actions palette. Of course, you could also record an action for a vertically centered guide and/or both horizontally and vertically centered guides.

CHANGE GUIDE DIRECTION

As in many applications, you can add non-printing guides to a document by clicking on one of the rulers and dragging onto the document. As you click on a ruler and drag a guide onto the document, the guide will be based on the ruler you've used (top ruler creates horizontal guides, side ruler creates vertical guides). To override this, press the Option key (PC: Alt key) as you drag from the ruler and you'll get the opposite guide. (Press and release Option/Alt to switch back and forth.)

Horizontal guide pulled from top ruler

Guide changed to vertical using this tip

©ISTOCKPHOTO/JENNIFER BORTON

MAKE GUIDES FROM OBJECTS

Not satisfied with only horizontal or vertical guides (and why should you be)? Then make your own. Create any object you want to use as a guide, make sure it is selected, and then from the View menu choose Guides>Make Guides (or press Command-5 [PC: Control-5]). To turn your guide back to a regular object, first unlock the guide using Command-Option-; (PC: Control-Alt-;), then use View>Guides>Release Guides (Command-Option-5 [PC: Control-Option-5]).

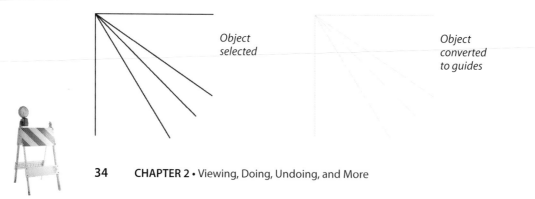

Object selected

Object converted to guides

LOCK A GUIDE TO AN OBJECT

If you want to have a guide that is locked to an object so that the guide moves with that object, here's the secret. Create and position a path that you'll use as the guide with either the Pen tool (P) or Line tool (\). Select the path and the other object(s) and press Command-G (PC: Control-G) to group all the objects together. Deselect everything (Command-Shift-A [PC: Control-Shift-A]), and then use the Direct Selection tool (A) to select only the path that you want as a guide. Press Command-5 (PC: Control-5) to convert the path to a guide. From then on, the guide will move with the group.

Path and
object grouped

Path as guide
locked to object

CHANGE LOCKED GUIDE INTO A PATH

To quickly change a locked guide into an editable path, hold down Command-Shift (PC: Control-Shift) and double-click on the guide. One very practical way to make use of this shortcut is when you want to adjust a guide. Use this shortcut, move the guide, then press Command-5 (PC: Control-5) to turn it back into a guide.

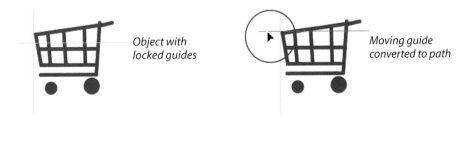

Object with
locked guides

Moving guide
converted to path

LOCK EVERYTHING ELSE

If you have one or more objects selected and you want to lock everything else, you can do that in one easy step. After selecting the object(s) you want to keep unlocked, press Command-Option-Shift-2 (PC: Control-Alt-Shift-2). To unlock everything, press Command-Option-2 (PC: Control-Alt-2).

©SCOTT WEICHERT

GET A NEW PERSPECTIVE ON GUIDES

In a previous tip, you saw how you can turn any object into a guide. Take this a step further and start using guides as a perspective grid. Just draw straight lines that match the perspective of the objects you'll be drawing. Once you're happy with your perspective grid, turn the lines into guides by choosing View>Guides>Make Guides. Then you can ensure that you'll be drawing to proper perspective throughout your illustration. You can even turn on Smart Guides (Command-U [PC: Control-U]) to help you align your paths to this new perspective grid.

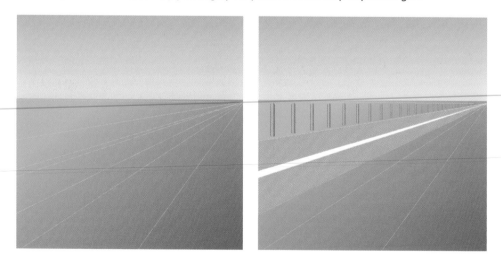

AUTO ADD RULERS TO EVERY NEW DOCUMENT

If you use rulers often in Illustrator and get frustrated by having to add them into each new document, then this tip is for you. You can automatically add rulers to each new document by modifying the Illustrator startup file located in your Applications or Program Files, in Adobe Illustrator CS2, in the Plug-ins folder. There are two files, so be sure to change both the CMYK and RGB files.

1. Quit Illustrator.

2. This step is optional. In the Adobe Illustrator CS2 Plug-ins folder, duplicate the current default startup file—Adobe Illustrator Startup_CMYK or Adobe Illustrator Startup_RGB—and give it a different name. (This creates a copy of the original startup file in case you need it again. You only need to do this once to back up the original if you want.)

3. Open one of the default startup files—Adobe Illustrator Startup_CMYK or Adobe Illustrator Startup_RGB—depending on which type of document you intend to use.

4. Choose View>Show Rulers.

5. Now, here's the trick. You can't just save this file because you haven't really made any changes that Illustrator will register yet. So, create a rectangle on the artboard using the Rectangle tool (M). Then just delete it.

6. Save the new file as Adobe Illustrator Startup _CMYK or Adobe Illustrator Startup_RGB (depending on which you opened) in the Plug-ins folder.

7. Restart Illustrator.

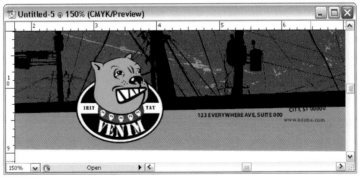

MEASURE FROM WHERE YOU WANT

By default, the rulers display with the top left of the page set to zero for the horizontal ruler, while the vertical ruler displays zero at the bottom left of the page. To change the ruler origin, click on the top left corner of the rulers and drag to wherever you want to set zero.

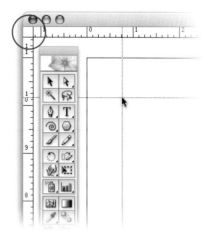

RESET THE RULERS

If you have changed the ruler origins and want to put them back to the default setting, double-click on the top left corner between the two rulers.

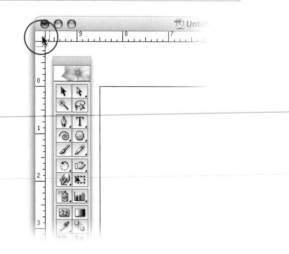

CHANGE RULER MEASUREMENT

The unit of measurement in Illustrator is determined in the Preferences (Illustrator>Preferences>Units & Display Performance [PC: Edit>Preferences>Units & Display Performance]). This will affect all aspects of the program that use measurements, including the rulers. However, if you need to quickly override the current measurements, just Control-click (PC: Right-click) anywhere on the ruler and choose your new unit of measurement.

MEASURE THE WAY YOU WANT

You set the default general unit of measurement in your Preferences (under the Units & Display Performance category) and that becomes the unit used by every dialog and palette (except Stroke and Type). It is possible, however, to override that default simply by typing in the unit you want to use. For example, if your default is set to inches, you can create a rectangle that's 40 points wide by clicking once with the Rectangle tool (M) on the artboard and then typing "40 pt" in the dialog. Use these shortcuts: in for inches, cm for centimeters, pt for points, px for pixels, or mm for millimeters.

MULTIPLE TOOLS?

Any tool in the Toolbox that displays a small triangle in the bottom right-hand corner has a set of "hidden" tools that can be popped up by clicking-and-holding on the current tool. Instead of popping up hidden tool menus all the time, make your life easier by tearing off commonly used tool menus. Just click-and-hold on the tool to pop up the other tool choices, and then drag over to the bar at the end of the tool menu. When you release the mouse, the tool menu becomes a floating palette that you can position anywhere you want. If you're really efficient (lazy?) you can add multiple tool menus all over the place. Tear off tool menus and position them all over the screen. This way, if you have a large monitor, you can always have a Type tool nearby without moving too far.

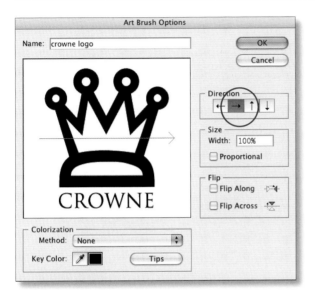

YOUR LOGO READY ANYTIME

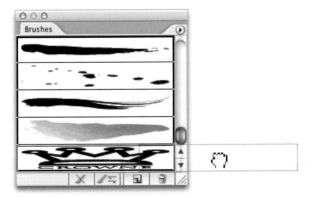

Here's a simple way to have your logo (or any other art you need) readily available in every new document you create. Open either the CMYK or RGB Adobe Illustrator Startup file (found in Illustrator CS2>Plug-ins) and paste your logo into that document. Select your logo (if it has text, you'll have to create an outline by going to Type>Create Outlines) and from the Brushes palette (under the Window menu) click on the New Brush icon. Choose New Art Brush as the type of brush and in the Art Brush Options dialog, click on the second Direction symbol so the arrow displays from left to right. Name your brush and click OK. Delete the artwork and save the document. From then on, you'll be able to click-and-drag the logo from the Brushes palette onto any new document.

SIMULATE PAPER COLOR

To help simulate what your artwork would look like printed on colored paper, you can change the color of the artboard. From the File menu, choose Document Setup and navigate to the Transparency category. In the View section, click on the top swatch to choose your paper color, then check Simulate Colored Paper. Click OK and the entire artboard will display in your chosen color. This eliminates the need to draw a separate box filled with the paper color. *Note:* The simulated paper will not display properly if you choose Show Transparency Grid from the View menu.

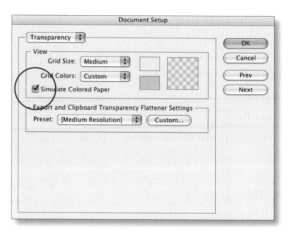

©CHRISTIAN MUSSELMAN

SHOW/HIDE CENTER POINT

Some objects, such as rectangles and ellipses, always show the center point, while others, such as polygons, do not. You can choose whether or not to show the center point using the Attributes palette in the Window menu. With the object selected, look in the Attributes palette and click on the small Show Center or Don't Show Center icon. This does not change the default setting for that tool. Instead, you'll have to do this for each object.

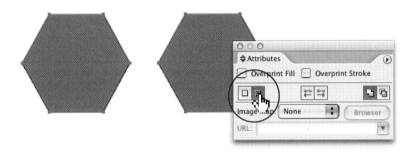

ANGLED GRID

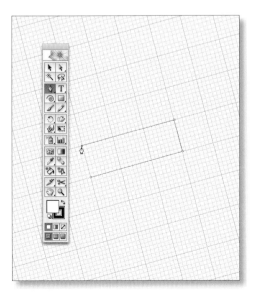

You can show a non-printing grid by using View>Show Grid, or by pressing Command-" (PC: Control-"). Once the grid is showing, there's no rule that says it must be perfectly horizontal—why not angle the grid to help you create angled objects? Just go to the Preferences dialog by pressing Command-K (PC: Control-K) and change the Constrain Angle field from zero degrees to whatever angle you want your grid to follow. Hold down the Shift key to force tools to precisely follow the angled grid. Once you're done, put it back to zero.

CHAPTER 2 • Viewing, Doing, Undoing, and More   **43**

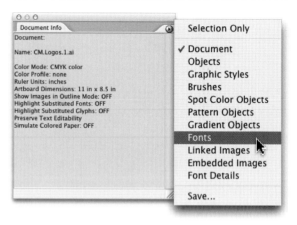

EVERYTHING YOU WANTED TO KNOW ABOUT...

Your document. Want to know what fonts you used, how many objects there are, or if images are linked or embedded? Try the Document Info palette, found under the Window menu. Then use the flyout menu to access all kinds of information about your document. You can even save the information as a text file by choosing Save, in the flyout menu.

GET OBJECT INFO

To see a quick summary of everything you need to know about a selected object, use the Document Info palette (Window>Document Info), and choose Selection Only from the flyout menu. Go back to the flyout menu to view other options such as Spot Color Objects, Fonts, Linked Objects, or to save a text file containing all the information.

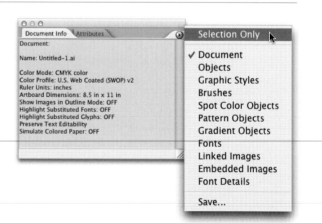

ACTIONS WITHIN ACTIONS

If you've recorded some actions for key operations, you can make use of these actions in another action. Confused? Here's an example: You have previously recorded an action that scales, rotates, and copies a selected object. Now you want to build on those steps and add to them. Rather than re-creating these steps, the first thing you record in the new action is to play the existing action. (Click the Create New Action icon, play the actions you want, then stop recording.) Simply put, you create an action that plays one or more actions. (It's easier than it sounds—try it, you'll like it!)

SAVE THAT VIEW

If you find yourself zooming in and out and scrolling a lot in a document, try saving specific views. To do this, simply change to the view you wish to save by zooming in or out and positioning your view. Then from the View menu choose New View, name the view, and from then on that view will be available at the bottom of the View menu. You can even create views that are in Outline mode rather than the Preview mode. The views you create are saved with the document itself (they are specific to that document as opposed to being global views).

TWO VIEWS, ONE DOCUMENT

It's often tempting to zoom way in to look at fine details in your document—remember, Illustrator lets you zoom in to 6,400%. At the same time, it's easy to get carried away and zoom in more than you need, or at least more than the naked eye can see. Here's one way to have the best of both worlds. Create a second view of your document

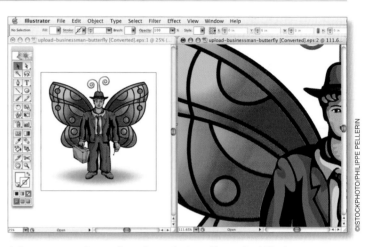

and keep it at Actual Size while you zoom in on the other window. From the Window menu, choose New Window, then manually adjust the window sizes so you can see both windows and pick a zoom level for each window.

PINPOINT IN THE NAVIGATOR

One of the advantages of using the Navigator palette (found under the Window menu) is that no matter how big your document is, you'll always see a thumbnail view in the Navigator. The red box indicates the portion of the document you are currently viewing in your window. To take full advantage of this thumbnail view and zoom in to a specific location in the document, hold down the Command key (PC: Control key) and click-and-drag in the Navigator thumbnail view. To return to a smaller view, Command-click (PC: Control-click) on the thumbnail again.

HIDE AND SHOW PALETTES

To make more room to work, temporarily hide the floating palettes by pressing the Tab key (with any tool active other than a Type tool). The Tab key acts like a toggle switch, so to show the palettes again, press Tab again. The only problem is that the Toolbox disappears too, so if you want to keep the Toolbox and hide the rest of the palettes, press Shift-Tab. As before, press the same shortcut to show the palettes again. (This is a better method than the alternative, which is spending all your time dragging palettes around to get them out of the way.)

©DAVID POUNDS

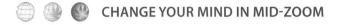

CHANGE YOUR MIND IN MID-ZOOM

If you start to click-and-drag with the Zoom tool (Z) to zoom in on a specific area and then realize you've positioned your mouse in the wrong place, don't let go of the mouse button. Press-and-hold the Spacebar, reposition your cursor, then let go of the Spacebar to continue selecting the zoom area. Once you try this one, you'll find yourself using it more often than you think.

THE ONE-SLIDE SLIDE SHOW

To present your artwork without the distraction of floating palettes and menus, follow these steps: From the View menu, choose Hide Artboard, then go back to the View menu and choose Hide Page Tiling. Now press the Tab key followed by F and F again. Tab hides all the palettes and pressing F cycles through full-screen views, one of which is Full Screen mode with no menus. If the rulers are showing, press Command-R (PC: Control-R) to hide them. (You can still use the Hand tool [H] to position your graphics, or use your zoom shortcuts to change your magnification.) To return to Standard Screen mode, press Tab and F, and then from the View menu show whatever else you want (rulers, artboard, page tiling, etc.).

Before   *After*

REMEMBER ONE PALETTE SHORTCUT

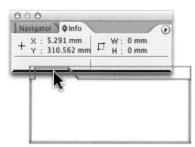

If you are having a hard time remembering keyboard shortcuts to show and hide all the floating palettes, focus on one shortcut. Pick a palette shortcut that you do remember (such as F8 for Info), and then dock other palettes into that one. To do this, click on the palette tab and drag onto the bottom of the chosen palette until a solid line appears. This will dock the palettes together, and now the one shortcut will hide and show multiple palettes at once.

ZOOM TOOL SHORTCUT

©ISTOCKPHOTO/ANDREY KRASNOV

Rather than moving all the way over to the Toolbox to click on the Zoom tool, press Command-Spacebar (PC: Control-Spacebar). This will interrupt whatever tool you are using and activate the Zoom tool. Click to zoom in, and then release the keys to return to whatever tool you were using. To zoom out, add the Option key (PC: Alt key), making the shortcut Command-Option-Spacebar (PC: Control-Alt-Spacebar).

HAND TOOL SHORTCUT

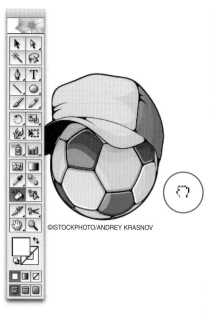

©ISTOCKPHOTO/ANDREY KRASNOV

Don't bother clicking on the Hand tool in the Tool-box to scroll your view, either. Just hold down the Spacebar. This will activate the Hand tool so you can scroll, then let go of the Spacebar to continue with your current tool. This works with all tools except the Type tools. (There is a trick, but you'll have to peek at the text chapter.)

KEEP ONLY SELECTED OBJECTS

As a quick way to hide all the objects you're not currently working on, try this: Select the object or objects you want to work on, then press Command-Option-Shift-3 (PC: Control-Alt-Shift-3). All the unselected objects will be hidden. To show all objects again, press Command-Option-3 (PC: Control-Alt-3).

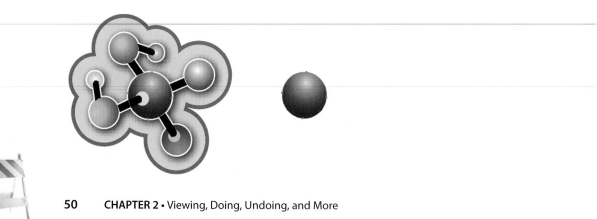

 **BE PRECISE**

If you want a more precise cursor, press the Caps Lock key. For many (but not all) tools, the tool cursor will change to a crosshair. To switch back to the regular tool cursors, release the Caps Lock key. Here's another way to look at this: If you use a tool and suddenly it isn't looking like the normal tool icon anymore, chances are the Caps Lock key is on. Turn off Caps Lock and there's your tool icon again.

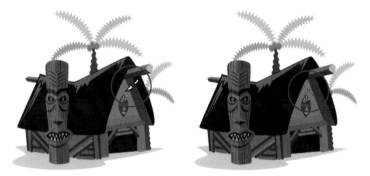

 **FRONT AND CENTER**

To ensure that an object is exactly centered on your page, use the Align palette (Window> Align or Shift-F7) with one minor change. From the palette's flyout menu, choose Align to Artboard. Then click on the Horizontal and Vertical Align Center icons to align your selected object to the page.

SEEING RED

If you're working on artwork that contains lots of red, the red View Box in the Navigator palette (Window>Navigator) might be a little difficult to see. In this situation (or if you just don't like the color red), you can change the color of the View Box by using the flyout menu in the Navigator palette and choosing Palette Options. In the resulting dialog, choose the color you'd like to use for the View Box.

ADD THE UNRECORDABLE

There are some functions that cannot be recorded in an action—such as painting tools, tool options, effects, view commands, and preferences. (In action-speak these are called unactionable.) To add these functions into an action, click the Create New Action icon in the Actions palette (Window>Actions), and choose Insert Menu Item from the palette's flyout menu to record non-recordable operations. With the Insert Menu Item dialog open, go to the menu command you'd like to use and it will be added automatically in the dialog.

HIDE YOUR GUIDES IN ONE CLICK

Although it is possible to hide/show guides with the shortcut Command-; (PC: Control-;), you can give yourself even more control by putting guides on their own layer. Click the Create New Layer icon in the Layers palette (under the Window menu), name the layer "guides," and then add guides to that layer. Then you can hide the guides by clicking on the Eye icon beside the layer name. To take this a step further, you could create several guide layers to give yourself even more options over which guides you'd like to be visible.

FREE RESOURCES

If you need some tips or tutorials, or you would like to download brushes, symbols, styles, actions, etc., check out the downloads through the Adobe Studio Exchange website: www.adobe.com/studio/main.html. Click on Adobe Studio Exchange on the left side of the screen and choose the downloads you're interested in from the pop-up menu.

 ### BACK TO BASICS

You may encounter situations when Illustrator starts behaving strangely. For example, tools aren't working the way they should or colors or patterns aren't displaying properly. In cases like this, you probably need to reset the Illustrator Preferences. Although it is possible to find the file and delete it, there is an easier way, especially since you need to launch Illustrator to create new preferences anyway. To reset the preference settings as you launch Illustrator CS2, hold down Command-Option-Shift (PC: Control-Alt-Shift). *Note:* Unlike previous versions, no dialog will appear, but the settings will be reset.

 ### DON'T SQUINT, CLICK

Having trouble focusing in on those tiny little fields in a palette? Instead, just click on the name of the field and it will highlight. Then type away and you're all set!

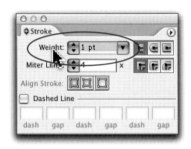

NEW DOCUMENT THE SAME AS LAST TIME

To create a new document with the same settings (width, height, orientation, color mode) as the last document you created, press Command-Option-N (PC: Control-Alt-N).

 ## RESET THE PAGE

 You can use the Page tool (nested under the Hand tool in the Toolbox) to set the page tiling in a document—wherever you position the mouse will be the bottom left corner of the page tiling (this also represents the printable area on your printer). If you've experimented with the Page tool and you want to get the page tiling back to "normal" (i.e., centered relative to the page), double-click on the Page tool in the Toolbox.

©SCOTT WEICHERT

 ## CHANGE TOOLS QUICKLY

There are many sets of tools that you access in the Toolbox by pressing-and-holding on the visible tool, which pops up a menu of additional tools. Another method to switch quickly between tools in a set is to hold down the Option key (PC: Alt key) and click on the visible tool. Each time you click, you'll switch to the next tool in the set.

 **MULTIPLE PAGES?**

Some people wish that they could create multipage documents in Illustrator. Well, with quite a bit of effort, you can (if you have Acrobat Distiller). First, go to File>New to create a document that is the size of all your pages side by side. For example, a four-page letter-size document would be set up as a landscape page with a width of 34 inches (8.5 x 4) and a height of 11 inches. Either choose View>Show Page Tiling or create guides to help you show the separation of the pages. Once you've finished designing your "superpage" and are ready to turn it into a multipage document, go to File>Print and in the Media section choose your orientation (we use Letter for Size, and in the Orientation section check the Portrait Up icon). Go to the Setup category (in the list on the left side of the dialog) and set the Tiling to Tile Full Pages. Then create a Postscript file by changing the Printer pop-up menu to Adobe PostScript File. (*Note:* You may need to change your PPD pop-up menu to select the correct print driver, depending on your system's setup.) Click the Save button and give the file a name followed by ".ps" as the file extension. Now launch Acrobat Distiller, open your saved PS document, and the Distiller will save the PDF file as a multipage document.

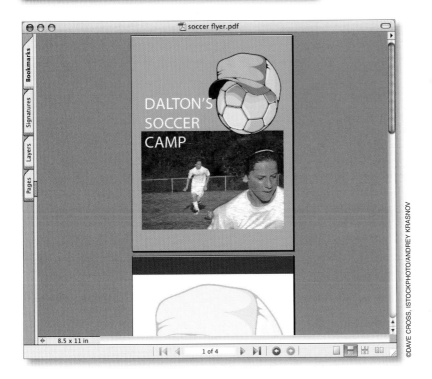

Tool Time

CREATING IN
ILLUSTRATOR CS2

You can never have enough tools. The more tools you have at your disposal, the more options you have for constructing your

Tool Time
creating in illustrator CS2

job. Just the other day, Matt was at The Home Depot considering what tools were missing from his collection—tools that would make his life easier. You're probably expecting me to cleverly relate this to using Illustrator's tools, but I really wasn't planning to. I just wanted to talk about our fascination with power tools and the tools we hope to get someday. In fact, just in case you're feeling generous, I can happily provide our wish list of dream tools. Meanwhile, I guess we'll have to make do with this collection of tips on using Illustrator's tools to create stuff (as I imagine, I can hear the sweet sound of a radial saw and smell the aroma of freshly cut pine).

PHOTO INSIDE OF TYPE

To fill text with a photo and keep the text editable, place an image into Illustrator (File>Place),
then create some text with the Type tool (T)
and position it on top of the photo. With the
Selection tool, select both the photo and
the type, and from the Object menu, select
Clipping Mask>Make, or press Command-7
(PC: Control-7). (In our example, we added a
stroke by selecting the text with the Selection tool and changing the Stroke color in the
Toolbox to black to make the type easier to see.)
Use the Type tool to edit the text or the Direct
Selection tool (A) to move the photo. To cancel
the effect completely, select the photo and text,
then go back to the Object menu and choose
Clipping Mask>Release. Let's review the most important aspect of this technique: The masking object (in this case, the text) needs to be on top.

©DAVE CROSS

START WITH A FONT

Stuck for a design idea, or searching for some clip art? Why not check out your built-in symbol
fonts such as Webdings, Dingbats, etc.? Get the Type tool (T) and click-and-drag out a text box.
Choose a font type and pick a large size. Open the Glyphs palette (Window>Type>Glyphs)
and use this palette to pick the shape (letter) you want to use. Once you've found a design you
like, double-click on it to add it to the text box. Then, select the symbol in the text box with the
Selection tool and from the Type menu, choose Create Outlines (or press Command-Shift-O
[PC: Control-Shift-O]). Use the Direct Selection tool (A) to edit and work with the object(s).

MAPPING MADE EASY

Looking for high-resolution maps and don't want to create your own? Planiglobe.com is a website that can generate them for you. You can generate maps interactively, zoom in and out, search for places, and add your own locations to a map. The PS and .ai versions (which you can download) are compatible to the PostScript® Level 1 language and the Illustrator® 7.0 format, respectively.

FIND YOUR FAVORITE LOGO?

This site is actually on our Most Valuable list. It's called Brandsoftheworld.com and can be found at, you guessed it, www.brandsoftheworld.com. The site is intended for browsing and exchange of the world's famous brand logos. The main goal behind the website is to enable designers to access vector forms of well-known brand logos that they can use in their presentations, given the permission of the copyright owner. The website also enables designers to upload their own works and professional details. Check it out—you'll love it!

 **CHANGE STAR SHAPE, PART ONE**

When you click-and-drag with the Star tool (nested under the Rectangle tool in the Toolbox) to create a star (duh), the distance between the outer radius (Radius 1) and inner radius (Radius 2) remains constant (Star 1). To experiment with the star shape, start to drag with the Star tool, then press-and-hold the Command key (PC: Control key). The inner radius will remain constant, so as you drag outward, you'll create longer points on the star (Star 2). Keep in mind that from then on, every subsequent star will have the same relationship between the two radii. To change this, you'll have to click once, enter a new value for Radius 2 and click OK (you can delete the star if you like).

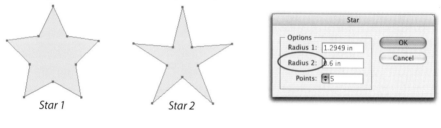

Star 1   *Star 2*

 **CHANGE STAR SHAPE, PART TWO**

Try this one at your own risk—it's very cool, but it can also make the Star tool act strangely from then on, so make sure you read the "how to get back to normal" part of this tip. Ready? Click-and-drag with the Star tool and don't let go throughout this whole procedure. Press the Down Arrow key to make a three-pointed star. Tap the Command and Option keys (PC: Control and Alt keys), then press the Up Arrow key to get multiple-point multi-stars (the star will continue to change each time you hit the Up Arrow key). To experiment even further, press-and-hold the Command key (PC: Control key) to play with the radius (as in the previous tip). The Star tool will create unusual stars like this from now on, so here's how to get it back to normal. Start to drag and tap the Command and Option keys (PC: Control and Alt keys) to get back to one star. You may also need to hit the Down Arrow key to return to a five-pointed star and drag while pressing-and-holding the Command key (PC: Control key) to get back to a more typical radius.

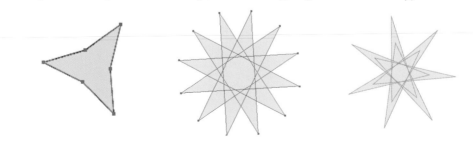

SEND UP A FLARE

The Flare tool (nested under the Rectangle tool in the Toolbox) creates its design in a couple of steps. First, click-and-drag to create the flare and its rays from the center outward. If you like, continue to hold down the mouse and press the Up or Down Arrow keys to change the number of rays. Once you release the mouse, the flares are done and you can move on to the rings. Position the mouse where you want the large ring to be positioned and click. If you're not satisfied, use the undo command (Command-Z [PC: Control-Z]) to undo just the rings. Position the mouse again and, for a bit of variety, click-and-hold the mouse as you press the tilde key (~) to randomize the rings. (Oh, and if you haven't figured this out already, flares look better when they appear on top of a darker shape.)

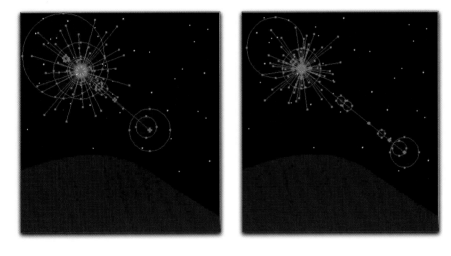

PERMANENT PATHFINDER

By default, clicking on the top row of icons in the Pathfinder palette creates a "live" effect that can be edited. Clicking on the Expand button makes the effect "permanent." If you want to create a permanent effect right away, press-and-hold the Option key (PC: Alt key) as you click on the Pathfinder icons of your choice.

 **SPRAY ON, SPRAY OFF**

To add symbols to a document, choose a symbol from the Symbols palette (under the Window menu), then use the Symbol Sprayer tool (Shift-S) to add symbols where you want them. With the Symbol Sprayer tool active, you can remove the active symbol by pressing-and-holding the Option key (PC: Alt key), which effectively turns the Symbol Sprayer tool into a symbol eraser.

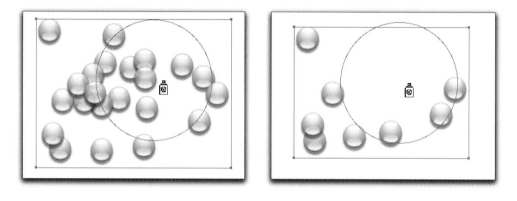

 **YEARS IN GRAPH DATA**

Here's a challenge: You've entered data to create a graph, and you've labeled the information with the year for each column of data. Problem is, Illustrator sees the year as part of the data and will include it in the graph. Solution? Surround the year with quotation marks in the Graph Data palette (Object>Graph>Data), and Illustrator will use it as a label rather than as part of the chart data.

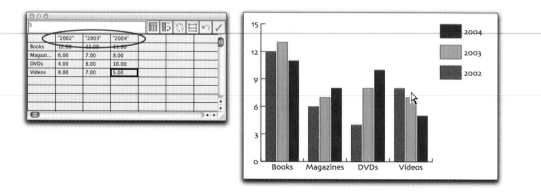

 **THAT'S OUT OF ONE HUNDRED**

By default, the value axis on a graph will be slightly more than the largest value in your data. To set a specific maximum value (such as 100), select the graph, and go to Object>Graph> Type. In the dialog, choose Value Axis from the pop-up menu at the top. Check the Override Calculated Values box and enter the maximum value (100 in our example). *Note:* The maximum value you choose will become the default, so be prepared to change it back the next time you create a graph.

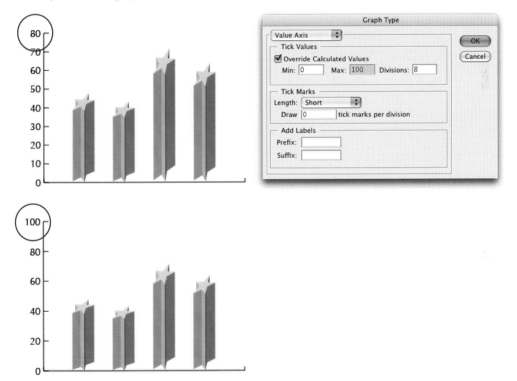

EDIT GRAPH DESIGNS

Illustrator comes with some pretty good graphic designs that you can use to replace the plain old columns created by the graph tools. In your computer's Applications folder (PC: Program Files folder), in Adobe Illustrator CS2>Cool Extras>Sample Files folder, choose the Graph Designs folder, and open one of the documents called Column & Marker Designs. To edit an existing design, go to the Object menu and choose Graph>Design. In the dialog, select the design from the list, click the Paste Design button, and then click OK. Edit the design, select it, and then use the same command, but this time click the New Design button to create a new column design. Name your design and click OK. (*Hint:* The column designs that contain a plus sign beside their names are sliding column designs [see next tip]). Save and close the design document. To apply a column design to a selected graph, use this command: Object>Graph>Column. Now pick your new design!

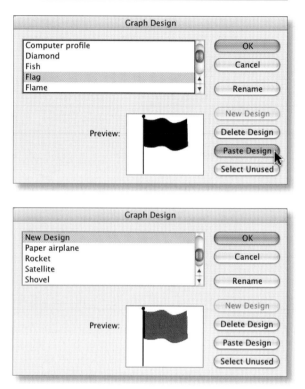

 ## SLIDING GRAPH DESIGNS

One of the most effective graph elements is a sliding column design. For example, use a martini glass as a column design where the top and bottom of the glass remain the same but the middle portion slides to grow taller. To do this, create your glass design and use the Pen tool (P) to create a horizontal line to indicate where the sliding should take place. Select the artwork and the line, then group them (Command-G [PC: Control-G]). Use the Direct Selection tool (A) to select the sliding line and from the View menu choose Guides>Make Guides. Then select the entire design and from the Object menu select Graph>Design. In the dialog, click the New Design button and use the Rename button if you want to call it something other than "New Design." To replace your graphic with this sliding design, select the graph and use Object>Graph>Column. In the dialog, choose your new design and from the Column Type pop-up menu choose Sliding. Here's a comparison of the difference between sliding and scaling column designs.

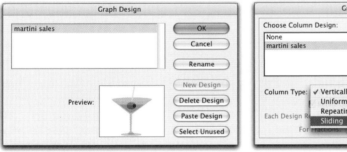

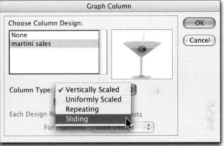

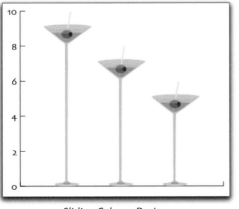

Sliding Column Design

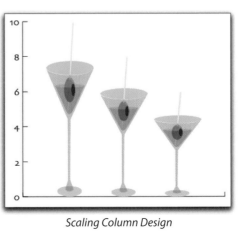

Scaling Column Design

DRAG-AND-DROP INSTEAD OF COPY-AND-PASTE

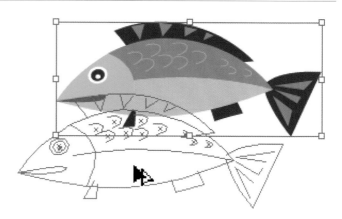

If you need to make a copy of an object, don't copy-and-paste (you could, but that's the slow way because you then have to move the pasted object where you want it). Instead, just press-and-hold the Option key (PC: Alt key) as you drag the object with the Selection tool (V) and you'll make a copy and position it in one step. If you want to make a copy perfectly aligned with the original, after you've started dragging, press-and-hold the Shift key, in addition to the Option key (PC: Alt key).

CHANGE TOOL SETTINGS ON THE FLY

As you drag the mouse to create shapes with tools such as the Star, Polygon, and Spiral tools (nested under the Rectangle tool on the Toolbox), use the Up and Down Arrow keys to increase or decrease the number of points, sides, or segments as you draw the shape. Here we used the Down Arrow key as we dragged out a shape with the Polygon tool.

MAKE YOUR OWN SPIROGRAPH

With many of the drawing tools, you can create multiple shapes by holding down the tilde key (~) as you drag. It's an interesting way to create wire frame shapes—or a computerized spirograph. (*Note:* Make sure you let go of the tool before you let go of the tilde key, or all of your wire framework will disappear and you'll be left with one object.)

CONVERT TO SHAPE

Here's a cool way to add a box to text without having to make a separate shape. Select a text object with the Selection tool (V) and in the Appearance palette (Window>Appearance), choose Add New Fill from the flyout menu. Then go to the Effect menu and choose Convert to Shape>Rectangle. In the dialog, in the Relative section, enter how much larger than the text you want the rectangle. Change the text and the rectangle grows with the text. (*Hint:* If you can't see the text because of the box's color, double check the Appearance palette to make sure the Characters tab is above the Fill tab. Then highlight your text with the Type tool (T) to change its color. Here we use black text on a yellow-filled box.)

LET THE BLEND TOOL DO THE MATH

Like a built-in calculator, the Blend tool (W) can do a form of calculation for you. For example, you draw two lines some distance apart, and now you want five more lines evenly spaced between the two original lines. Rather than doing any math to figure out how far apart to space the lines, just create a blend between the two objects. With the Blend tool, click on one line, avoiding anchor points. Then, Option-click (PC: Alt-click) on the other line. In the dialog, enter the number of new lines you want for the specified steps. Illustrator does the math and evenly spaces the new lines between the two originals. (And, since the effect is live, the spacing will automatically update if you move either of the two original objects, or change the angle of one of the lines.)

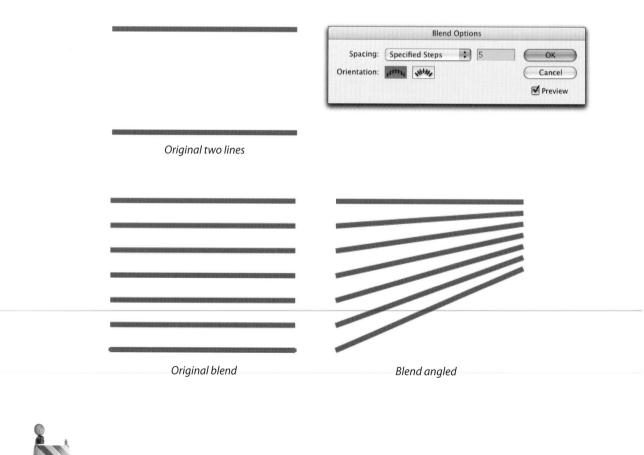

Original two lines

Original blend   *Blend angled*

MORE BLENDING

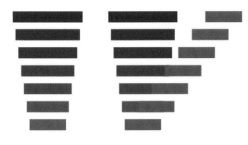

If you've created a blend between two objects and want to add to the blend, one way is to make a copy of the start or end object. Use the Direct Selection tool (A) with the Option key (PC: Alt key) held down, and drag a copy of the object. As you let go, the blend will be updated to include the newly copied object (using the same number of blend objects that are in the original blend).

YET MORE BLENDING

Here's another way to add to an existing blend using any shape you want. Create the shape you want to add to the blend and then go to the Layers palette. Find the Blend and click on the triangle to show its sublayers. Click on the new object and drag it to the Layers palette into the blend's sublayers. The blend will be determined by the position of the new object, so find the object in the palette and drag it to the top of the blend layers. This will make a new blend between it and the last object in the original blend. A middle position redraws the blend with the new object in the middle of the original blend. Positioning it at the bottom of the blend layers means the new blend will form between the new object and the first object in the original blend.

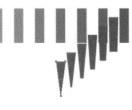

BEND THE BLEND

Here's how to take a blend and turn it up a notch. After creating a blend, draw a path for the blend to follow. Shift-click with the Selection tool (V) to select the path and the entire blend (all the objects in the blend), and from the Object menu choose Blend>Replace Spine. The straight line between the first and last objects in the blend will be replaced with your path. If the objects are not evenly spaced out along the path, see the next tip.

SHAPES AROUND A CIRCLE

If you use a circular path for the Replace Spine command, chances are the objects in your blend will not be evenly distributed around the circle. There's a simple trick to make sure the objects in your blend are evenly spaced around the circle: Select the path, and with the Scissors tool (C) click somewhere on the path of the circle to create an open path (don't move anything, just click once to cut the path). The blended objects will automatically be distributed along the path. (*Note:* Try this for any path, not just circles.)

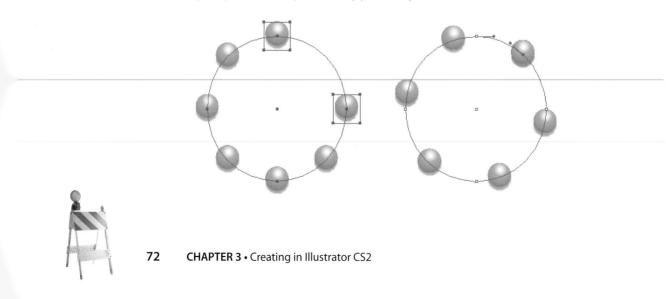

CHANGE THE BLEND

After you've created a blend (and it's still live), you can change the number of steps in the blend by going to the Object menu and choosing Blend>Blend Options (or double-clicking the Blend tool in the Toolbox). In the dialog, change the number of Specified Steps and the blend will update. An even quicker way is to check the Preview box at the bottom of the dialog, and use the Up and Down Arrow keys for an instant update.

OUTLINE STROKE

One simple way to make a shape that you can use as a building block to create your design, is to convert a path with a thick stroke into an object. Draw a path, add a thick stroke (Window>Stroke), and then from the Object menu choose Path>Outline Stroke. In our example, we then straightened the ends and made multiple copies.

WHITESIDE
BUILDING CONSULTANTS

LIVE TRACE NOT WORKING HOW YOU'D LIKE? TRY THIS

If you've imported a number of sketches into Illustrator and have tried to run Live Trace (under the Object menu) on them, you may have realized it doesn't always work as good as you'd like. You can try to change the Tracing Options to better fit the sketch that you're tracing, but that still doesn't always do the trick. If that's the case, then try this: Duplicate the sketch layer (go to Window>Layer, and choose Duplicate from the Layer palette's flyout menu) and, on the Transparency palette, change the Blend Mode of the duplicate to Multiply. Then duplicate the layer copy a couple more times. Each time, you'll  see the sketch get darker and darker. However, since we can't run Live Trace on several layers at once, we have to flatten the artwork. First, press Command-A (PC: Control-A) to select all the layers. Then, choose Object>Rasterize. Don't worry about the resolution setting since you're just going to run Live Trace on this sketch anyway, just click OK. Now you'll be able to run Live Trace on this image and the results should look much better.

© PATRICK SHETTLESWORTH

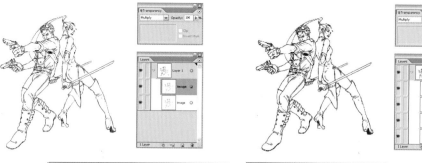

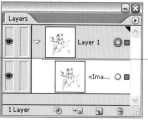

IS LIVE TRACE STILL NOT WORKING HOW YOU'D LIKE? TAKE IT A STEP FURTHER

Original Sketch

If the previous tip doesn't do the trick when working with Live Trace, then you may have to resort to some more extreme measures. Try opening the sketch in Photoshop. Choose Image> Adjustments>Levels to display the Levels dialog box. Try moving the black slider under Input Levels toward the right to darken the lines. When you're done, click OK, save the image, and import this sketch into Illustrator again. Using Levels in Photoshop will help give Illustrator more definition with which to trace the image and you should come out with a much better result.

Live Trace applied without Levels adjustment

Levels adjustment in Photoshop

Levels-adjusted sketch in Illustrator before Live Trace

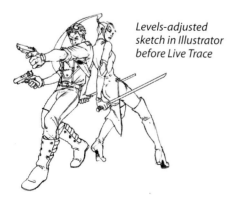

Live Trace applied to Levels-adjusted sketch

VIEWING REFERENCE PHOTOS WHEN USING THE MESH TOOL

Here's a great tip for working with the Mesh tool (U). Often, illustrators will use a reference photo as a starting place to create their work. Well, if you're using the Mesh tool, it can often be useful to switch between Outline and Preview modes because the colors you're adding may cover up the reference photo. Here's the tip: Be sure that when you bring your reference photo into Illustrator, that you place it as a template layer. This will ensure that you're able to view it in Outline mode. If not, when you switch to Outline mode, all you'll see are the outlines and no photo.

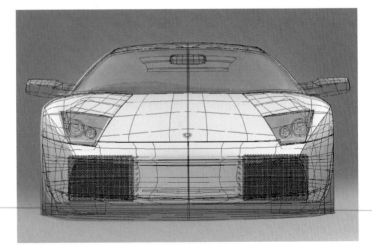

©MATT KLOSKOWSKI

GRADIENT BRUSHES

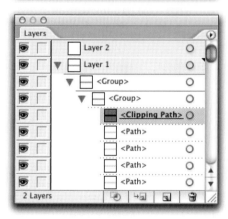

You can make gradients follow a path by making an art brush. Start by making a rectangle with the Rectangle tool (M) and change the fill to Gradient (the center thumbnail near the bottom of the Toolbox under the Fill and Stroke thumbnails). Use the Gradient and Color palettes (under the Window menu) to change the color and style of the gradient. (To add additional color stops, Option-click on a stop and drag it sideways.) From the Object menu, choose Expand. In the dialog, change the number of objects—the number you use will depend on the final use of the artwork, screen versus print. Make sure that no banding is visible once you've expanded the gradient, meaning there are no lines visible in the gradient. If there is banding, you'll have to undo (Command-Z [PC: Control-Z]) and try a higher number. Then in the Layers palette (found under the Window menu), scroll down the layer information until you see the object's clipping path and drag it to the palette's Trash icon. With the expanded gradient still selected, from the Brushes palette's flyout menu choose New Brush and select New Art Brush. Give your brush a name and select other options, such as direction and size. Now you have a gradient brush that you can apply to any path.

 **DIVIDE OBJECTS BELOW**

This one's a little odd since it breaks a fundamental rule of Illustrator: Make sure you have selected all the objects you want to work with. In the case of the command called Divide Objects Below, it won't work if more than one object is selected. Simply create the object that will do the dividing and position it over the other (filled) object(s) to be divided. Then choose Object>Path>Divide Objects Below. (If you have too many objects selected, it won't work and you'll get a warning dialog.)

 **CHANGE GRIDS ON THE FLY**

By default, the Rectangular Grid tool (nested under the Line tool in the Toolbox) creates equal spacing between the horizontal and vertical dividers. To change the spacing as you drag a grid, press X or C to move horizontal dividers left or right, and press V or F to move vertical dividers up or down. (Here we pressed C as we dragged out the grid.)

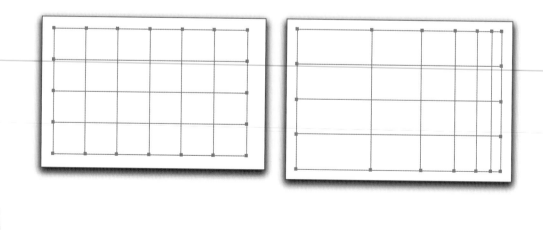

 **LIVE INTERLOCKING OBJECTS**

Using the Live Paint Bucket (K), you can easily create interlocking objects that remain live. Create two overlapping objects that have outlined paths (Object>Path>Outline Stroke), select them both, and click on the selected objects with the Live Paint Bucket to turn them into a Live Paint Object. Pick the color of one of the objects and click again with the Live Paint Bucket tool where the objects overlap. Now you can use the Direct Selection tool (A) to reposition either object while keeping the interlocking look.

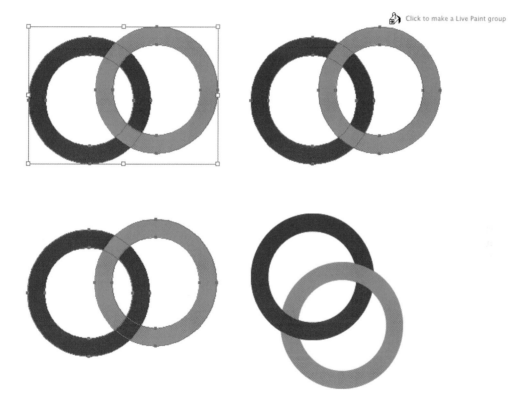

LIVE INTERLOCKING OBJECTS, PART 2

Okay, so it is a bit of a stretch to make this a separate tip, but frankly, it's just easier to separate this. Once you've created a Live Paint interlocking object like in our last tip, you can take it up a notch by applying the Effect>3D>Extrude & Bevel to the objects. They'll still be interlocked, you can reposition them, and they're in 3D!

CREATING WIREFRAMES

Ever see that cool black and white line view of your 3D objects when you're editing the lighting cube in the 3D effects dialog box? It's called a wireframe, and creating that effect in Illustrator CS2 is easier than ever. Just create an object and apply some 3D effect to it (Effect>3D>Extrude and Bevel or Revolve). At the bottom of the resulting 3D effect options dialog, change the Surface setting pop-up menu from Plastic to Wireframe, and you'll always have that effect instead of the default shaded view.

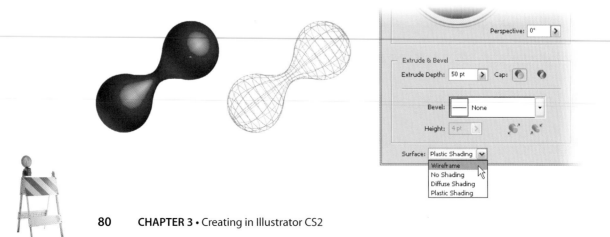

ADD TO A SHAPE TO CREATE A SHAPE

Sometimes it's easier to create a simple shape and then add to it with more anchor points. For example, to create a map pointer, draw a rectangle with the Rectangle tool (M) and then use the Add Anchor Point tool (+) to add three anchor points along the bottom. Press A to get the Direct Selection tool, then click-and-drag out the middle of the three anchor points you added. There you have it!

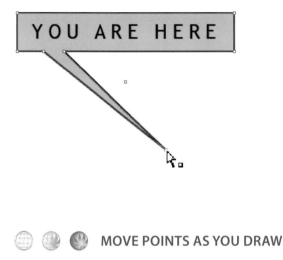

MOVE POINTS AS YOU DRAW

With the Pen tool (P), you can change your mind about the positioning of the anchor points as you draw. Without letting go of the Pen tool, press the Spacebar and drag to move the active anchor point. Let go of the Spacebar to continue drawing with the Pen tool.

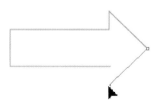

AUTO ADD/DELETE GETTING IN YOUR WAY

By default, Illustrator automatically adds or deletes a point on an existing path when you move the Pen tool (P) near it. However, this doesn't help much when you don't want to add or delete from the path, but instead want to create an entirely new path altogether. There is a preference setting to disable this, but there is also a quick way to disable it using the keyboard. Just hold down the Shift key when you're near the path and you see the cursor with the little plus sign next to it. Instead, you'll see the cursor with the small x next to it meaning you're going to start a new path altogether.

MULTIPLE OBJECTS AS A MASK

If you try to use more than one object as a clipping mask, only the last object you created will act as a mask—the others will be ignored. To use those multiple objects as a mask, you'll first have to select all the objects and from the Object menu, choose Compound Path>Make, or press Command-8 (PC: Control-8). Then position the compounded objects on top of the object you're masking, and use the Object>Clipping Mask>Make command, or press Command-7 (PC: Control-7).

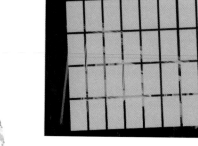

©DAVE CROSS

ROUND THOSE CORNERS

As you are dragging the Rounded Rectangle tool (nested under the Rectangle tool in the Toolbox) to create a rounded-corner rectangle (duh), you can change the radius (size) of the rounded corners. Just press the Up or Down Arrow key to increase or decrease the corner radius, or press the Left Arrow key to jump to the minimum radius or the Right Arrow key to change to the maximum radius. (The minimum radius is zero, while the maximum radius depends on the size of the rectangle you are creating. The "maximum" maximum radius is 8,192 points—ideal for those building-sized rectangles.)

SAME WIDTH AND HEIGHT

Click on the artboard with a tool to get the dialog where you can enter the width and height. To make the width and height both the same amount, enter your number in the width field, and then click on the word Height to use the same measurement.

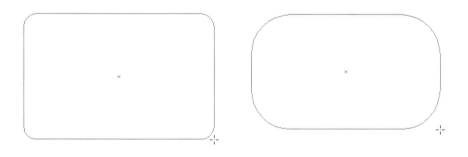

CHANGING ARCS

You can change the performance of the Arc tool by holding down a couple of keys. As you drag with the Arc tool (nested under the Line tool in the Toolbox), press C to switch between an open and closed arc (like we did here). Press F to flip the axis of the arc.

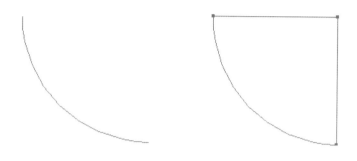

CLOSE A PATH AUTOMATICALLY

To create a closed path with the Paintbrush tool (B) or the Pencil tool (N), start drawing, then click-and-hold the Option key (PC: Alt key). Continue drawing, and when you're ready to have the path closed for you, let go of the tool. Once the path has closed, then release the Option key (PC: Alt key).

PRESERVE BRUSH STROKE OPTIONS

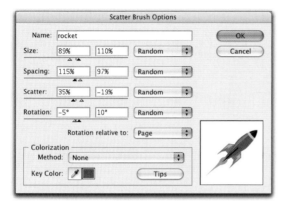

When you create a Scatter brush (go to Window>Brushes, and on the Brushes palette's flyout menu, choose New Brush, then Scatter Brush), you can set various options such as size, scatter amount, rotation, and more. If you apply a different Scatter brush to a stroke created with your new Scatter brush, you'll lose those brush options—unless you hold down the Option key (PC: Alt key) when you click on the new brush that you want to assign a brush stroke to.

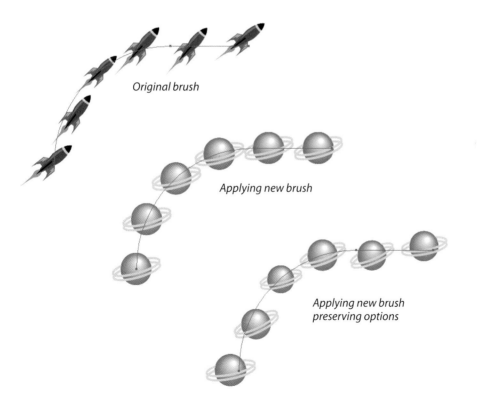

Original brush

Applying new brush

Applying new brush preserving options

DISABLE AUTO ADD/DELETE

By default, the Pen tool (P) automatically adds anchor points to an
existing path, and deletes existing
anchor points. In some situations,
that option may actually be a hin-
drance, especially if you're trying
to create a new path very close to
an existing path. To temporarily
make the Pen tool act as simply
a *Pen* tool, go to the Preferences
(Command-K [PC: Control-K])
and check the Disable Auto
Add/Delete box in the General
Preferences. As always, remember
to return the Pen to "normal" after
you're done.

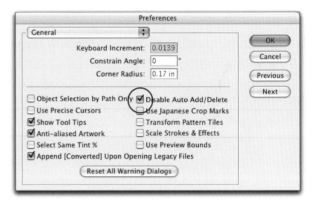

SPLIT INTO GRID

If you need to make a series
of rectangles that are evenly
spaced apart, draw a rectangle
in the overall width you need.
Then from the Object menu,
choose Path>Split Into Grid.
Click the Preview checkbox
and then enter the number of
rows to indicate the number of
objects you want. You can also
enter specific widths, gutters
(space between columns), or the
total width or height you need.
There is also the option of creating guides for your grid.

THE PERFECT STAR

If you start to draw a star (needless to say, with the Star tool that is nested under the Rectangle tool in the Toolbox), and the settings are not what you want, it's because the tool is remembering the last settings you used for the radius. To create the "perfect" star without having to change the settings, press-and-hold Option-Shift (PC: Alt-Shift) while clicking-and-dragging the star. Option/Alt changes the radius to the "ideal" setting for a perfect star and shift will ensure the sides of the star are straight.

TARGET PRACTICE

Need a series of circles, each slightly larger than the last? Here's a very simple method: Use the Polar Grid tool (found under the Line tool in the Toolbox). As you drag with the tool, use the Up or Down Arrow key to increase or decrease the number of circles. Use the Left or Right Arrow key to increase or decrease the number of dividers. You can always use the Direct Selection tool (A) to edit the results.

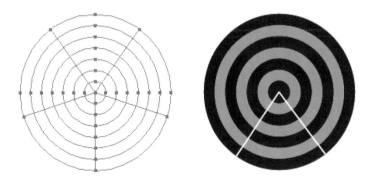

OPACITY MASKS

An opacity mask adds the ability to make portions of an object transparent. To create an opacity mask, draw an object filled with black or shades of gray and position it over the object to which you want to apply the mask (black completely hides objects, gray creates partial transparency). Select both objects and from the Transparency palette's flyout menu, choose Make Opacity Mask. Deselect the Clip checkbox. To temporarily disable the opacity mask, press-and-hold the Shift key and click on the mask thumbnail in the Transparency palette. To see the mask and edit it, press-and-hold the Option key (PC: Alt key) and click on the mask thumbnail. To return to the normal view, click on the object thumbnail (on the left in the palette).

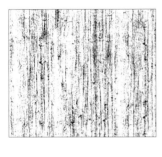

VINTAGE TEXTURE EFFECT

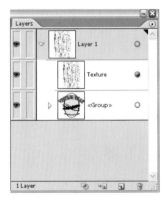

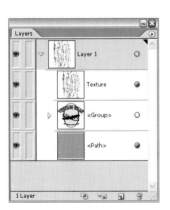

Have you ever seen that old vintage/weathered style t-shirt? It looks like it's been washed a thousand times but in reality it hasn't. How do you know? Because you can buy this style of a t-shirt today brand new and I'm betting that the manufacturer hasn't washed it that many times already. Anyway, it's a nice effect and can easily be added to any of your artwork using Illustrator. First, open any graphics that you'd like to apply this vintage effect to. Then group them together, so you just have one object to work with. Next, import a grayscale texture image from anywhere—it could have been created in Photoshop or scanned in on a flatbed scanner. Place the texture on a layer above the artwork that you want to add the vintage effect to. Then select both the texture layer and the group containing the artwork and choose Make Opacity Mask from the Transparency palette's flyout menu. All the areas that were black will now be the color of whatever is behind the grouped graphics (in this case the white artboard). If you want, you can add a rectangle in a layer below the group to change the color.

Nip/Tuck

SELECTING, EDITING, AND TRANSFORMING

*Back in the first version of Illustrator, the
Status Bar changed on the fly to give you
continuous feedback about the tools you were*

Nip/Tuck

selecting, editing, and transforming

*using. Why are we telling you this? A couple of
reasons: First, it establishes fake credibility since
no one can go back and check to see if this is
true or if we just completely made it up. Second,
we wanted to demonstrate the power of any
statement that starts, "Back in the first version
of Illustrator…" Got your attention, didn't it? As
a special bonus available only to you, the reader,
we're giving you the go-ahead to make claims
about the original Illustrator. You just never
know when it could come in handy. Hey, you
may even want to go for it and use something
like this: "Back when I used to copy artwork from
Illustrator 88 into the original Photoshop…" You'll
thank us later.*

SAVE A SELECTION

If you've made a challenging selection of a number of objects, you don't want to have to do that again, so save yourself the effort. With the objects selected, go to the Select menu and choose Save Selection. Give your selection an appropriate name and click OK. From then on, if you need to make that difficult selection, just choose it from the bottom of the Select menu. (If you have deleted one or more objects from the page, whatever objects remain in that saved selection will be selected.)

RESHAPE PATHS BY DRAWING

Use the Pencil tool (N) to reshape any existing path by drawing. Make sure the path is selected, then click-and-drag with the Pencil tool to redraw the path. You must start fairly close to the path for Illustrator to recognize that you are redrawing versus creating a new path. How close? That depends on the preference for the Pencil tool. Double-click on the Pencil tool in the Toolbox to set the distance from the path in the Options section of the dialog—just click Edit Selected Paths and choose your pixel amount.

RESHAPE PATHS BY PAINTING?

So, does this concept also work with the Paintbrush tool (B)? Well, kinda. The Paintbrush tool can only be used to reshape paths that were created with the Paintbrush tool (whereas the Pencil tool will reshape any path, including those created with the Paintbrush tool). Double-click the tool in the Toolbox to change its preferences, just like the Pencil tool (see previous tip).

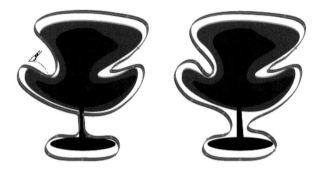

EDITING A TYPE PATH

It's easy enough to create type on a path in Illustrator. Just create a path, grab the Type tool (T), and click on the path to start aligning your type to it. However, once you do this, it appears as if your path is gone. Don't worry, it's not. Just switch to the Direct Selection tool (A), and click on the actual path. Don't click on the type, because that will just select the entire object. You want to make sure you click on the path to display any anchor points or directional handles. Then, you're free to manipulate the path just as you would any other path in Illustrator.

CUT OR ADD A POINT

When you are using the Scissors tool (C) to cut a path, you may want to add an anchor point or two to help edit the path. Rather than switching to the Pen tool (P) or the Add Anchor Point tool (+), just press-and-hold the Option key (PC: Alt key) and the Scissors tool will switch (temporarily) to the Add Anchor Point tool. Click on the path to add a point, then let go of the Option key to return to the Scissors tool.

JOIN VS. AVERAGE & JOIN

It's important to recognize the difference between Join and Average & Join. If you select the end-points of two paths with the Direct Selection tool (A) and choose Object>Path>Join (Command-J [PC: Control-J]), a straight path will be created to join the two paths. If you want the paths to be joined together using a common point, first choose Average (Command-Option-J [PC: Control-Alt-J]), then use Join.

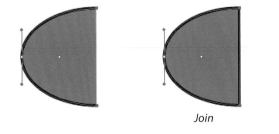

Join

Average and Join

AVERAGE AND JOIN IN ONE STEP

Average

Axis
- ◯ Horizontal
- ◯ Vertical
- ⦿ Both

OK

Cancel

As shown in the previous tip, to join two open paths using a common point, you select the end-points of both paths with the Direct Selection tool (A). Choose Average from the Object menu (Object>Path>Average), click Both for Axis in the resulting dialog, and then click OK to make the two anchor points share one location. Then it's back to the Object menu to choose Path>Join. To trim the process down to one step, just select the two end-points, press Command-Option-Shift-J (PC: Control-Alt-Shift-J) to Average and Join in one step.

THE TRUE CENTER

When you use the Attributes palette (Window>Attributes) to show the center of a star, you'll note that the center point isn't exactly centered. Rather than try to explain why this happens (which isn't really important since we can't change it), let's see how to find the true center of a star. Select the object, then choose Edit>Copy (Command-C [PC: Control-C]), and then Edit>Paste in Front (Command-F [PC: Control-F]). From the Object menu choose Path>Average (Command-Option-J [PC: Control-Alt-J]). In the dialog, click Both for Axis. The point that appears is the true center of the object.

BIGGER OR SMALLER A BIT AT A TIME

Perhaps you are trying to scale one object to fit within a second object, or you need to make an object smaller, but you're not sure by how much. Try this method: With the object selected, double-click on the Scale tool and enter 98% if you're scaling down, or 102% if you're making it larger. That will scale the object 2% smaller or larger. (You can choose Copy from the dialog to make a smaller or larger copy of your object, like we did in our example here.) Then press Command-D (PC: Control-D) to repeat the transformation. Each time you press this shortcut, the object will scale by 2% (smaller or larger, depending on the value you entered), allowing you to scale a bit at a time.

SCALE TOOL CLONING

Here's a neat trick when using the Scale tool (S). While you're scaling an object, try pressing-and-holding the Option key (PC: Alt key), and that will make a duplicate copy of the object for scaling instead of modifying the original. This just saves you the step of creating the duplicate first and lets you do it all in one step.

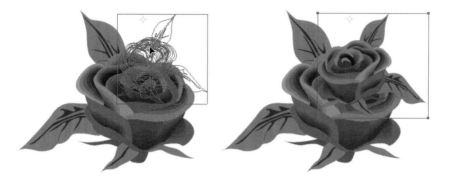

KEEP PROPORTIONS

When you use the Transform palette (Window>Transform) to change the size of an object, you can enter the width and the height for a selected object and press Return (PC: Enter). Another option is to enter either width or height and keep the other measurement proportionate by pressing Command-Return (PC: Control-Enter). For example, if your object is 1.5 inches high by 3 inches wide, change the width from 3 to 6 inches and press Command-Return (PC: Control-Enter), and the height will automatically change to 3 inches.

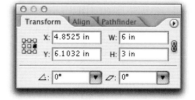

 **QUICK FLIP**

When you need to flip an object horizontally or vertically, ignore the Reflect tool and jump right to the Transform palette (Window>Transform). Select the object and from the palette's flyout menu, choose either Flip Horizontal or Flip Vertical.

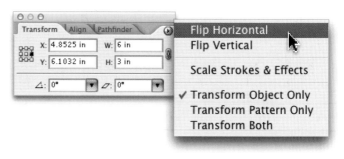

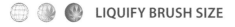 **LIQUIFY BRUSH SIZE**

When you are using any of the liquify tools (Warp, Twirl, etc.) and your brush is the wrong size, press-and-hold the Option key (PC: Alt key), and drag to change the size. Drag outwards to make the size larger, drag inwards to make it smaller. (*Note:* Using Option/Alt alone will alter the brush size non-proportionally. If you want to keep the brush as a perfect circle but change its size, use Option-Shift [PC: Alt-Shift].)

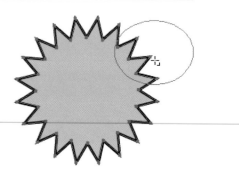

SELECT SAME, AGAIN

Select	Filter	Effect	View	Window	Help

All	⌘A
Deselect	⇧⌘A
Reselect	⌘6
Inverse	
Next Object Above	⌥⌘]
Next Object Below	⌥⌘[
Same ▶	
Object ▶	
Save Selection...	
Edit Selection...	
outer edge of building	
all type objects	
inner shading	

Blending Mode
Fill & Stroke
Fill Color
Opacity
Stroke Color
Stroke Weight
Style
Symbol Instance
Link Block Series

Use the Select>Same options to select objects that have the same Fill Color, Fill & Stroke, Blending Mode, etc. Then, the next time you need to make a selection using the same "select same" criteria, press Command-6 (PC: Control-6). (*Note:* If your selection requires a fill and/or stroke color(s), make sure you have those colors selected in the Toolbox.)

SELECT COLOR FROM SWATCHES

©ERWIN HAYA

If you want to see if you've used a specific color in your document—and if so, where—with nothing selected, click on the swatch in the Swatches palette and then use Select>Same> Fill Color and every object filled with that color will be selected (regardless of which layer they're on).

SELECTING GROUPS

Use the Direct Selection tool (A) to select individual paths and anchor points, even when they're part of a group. To select the entire path, press-and-hold the Option key (PC: Alt key) as you click on the path. To take this a step further, each time you click on the same path—with the Option key (PC: Alt key) held down—you will select the group that contains the path, and then the group that contains the group, and so on. You'll really have to try this one to see how useful it is!

SELECTING MESH POINTS EASILY

Here's a great tip when working with the Mesh tool (U). Many times, you'll need to select an existing mesh point to change its color or placement. Well, if you use the Mesh Tool to select points, you'll find that you wind up inadvertently adding a mesh point here or there because you didn't click on the exact point. Instead of using the Mesh tool for this, try pressing-and-holding the Command key (PC: Control key) and that'll switch to the Direct Selection tool (A). Now you won't have to worry about adding mesh points that you didn't want all over the place.

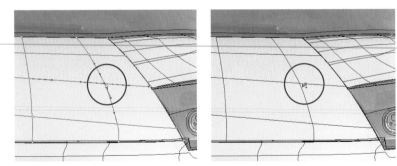

Clicking in the wrong place will inadvertently add a new mesh point

SELECTING MULTIPLE MESH POINTS EASILY

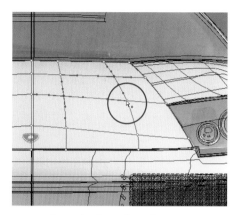

Take the previous tip a step further by adding the Shift key into the mix. While holding down the Command key (PC: Control key) to select certain points, hold down the Shift key to select multiple points. This comes in handy when you want to change the color of several mesh points at once.

Several points selected at once

LET ILLUSTRATOR CALCULATE IT FOR YOU

You can perform simple math in the Transform palette or the Control palette, both found under the Window menu. For example, if you need to make an object one-third of its width, just click after the current size in the Width field and type /3. Use / for divided by, * for multiplied by and + or - for, well, you know. Then press Return (PC: Enter) and Illustrator will do the calculation and transform accordingly.

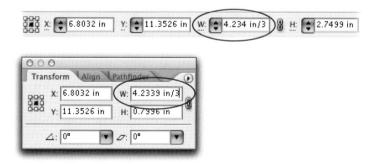

EDITABLE TRANSFORMATIONS

When you use any of the transformation tools such as Scale (S) or Rotate (R), the effect is permanent once you save and close the document. For example, rotate an object, save the document, and close it. Next time you reopen the document, there is no easy way to undo this change. Instead, consider using the Transform command under the Effect menu. You'll find it here: Effect>Distort & Transform>Transform. In the dialog, check the Preview option and then apply whatever transformation you like. Once you've clicked OK, you'll always be able to access and edit these transforma-

tions (even after closing the document) by selecting the object, looking in the Appearance palette, and double-clicking on Transform.

ROTATE WITH CARE

When you're using the Rotate tool (R), keep this in mind. If you leave the cursor too close to the original rotate bounding box, the results can be somewhat erratic. For more precise control, move the cursor farther away from the object you're rotating. That will give you more control over positioning it.

 **ROTATION BY THE NUMBERS**

To rotate and copy an object a specific number of times so you end up with even angles between objects, let Illustrator figure it out for you. Select your object, then with the Rotate tool (R), press-and-hold the Option key (PC: Alt key), and click on the bottom of the object. In the Rotate dialog, enter 360/x, with x being the number of objects you want. Then click Copy. The object will be copied and rotated the correct number of degrees. Then press Command-D (PC: Control-D) x-2 times (with x being the number you used before) to complete the effect. For example, for eight objects you'd enter 360/8 in the Rotate dialog, click Copy, and then press Command-D six times (since you already have the original and the first copy).

 **REPEAT LAST PATHFINDER**

Need to repeat the last Pathfinder effect you just used? Use the flyout menu in the Pathfinder palette (found under the Window menu) and choose Repeat (name of Pathfinder), or press Command-4 (PC: Control-4).

TRANSFORM BY NUMBER

With all transformation tools, such as Scale, Rotate, and Shear, you can transform manually by dragging the mouse or numerically. Double-click on any transformation tool to get a dialog for a numeric transformation. By default, the reference point for the transformation is the center of the object. But to open the dialog and set a different reference point, press-and-hold the Option key (PC: Alt key) and click in the spot you'd like to use as a reference point.

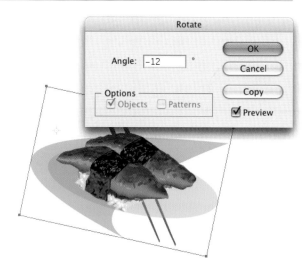

FREE TRANSFORM

Add all kinds of extra functions to the Free Transform tool (E) by using a number of different keys, after you click on a corner handle. For example, press-and-hold the Command key (PC: Control key) as you click-and-drag to distort; press Command-Option-Shift (PC: Control-Alt-Shift) to distort perspective; press Command-Option (PC: Control-Alt) to shear an object; press-and-hold Shift to scale; etc.

PICK THE BEST TRANSFORMATION

When you want to transform multiple objects, you have a couple of choices. One option is to select the objects and use transformation commands (Object>Transform), such as Scale or Rotate. This will transform the objects as if they were one object. The other choice is the Transform Each command (Object>Transform>Transform Each). Use this dialog to transform the separate objects, and take advantage of a preview.

SELECT BEHIND

©MIKE SELLERS/PHOTO © ABLESTOCK.COM

To select an object hidden behind another object, select the top object, and then press Command-Option-left bracket ([) (PC: Control-Alt-left bracket). That will select the next object, below the selected object. Keep pressing the same shortcut to select the next object down. To select back the other way (Select>Next Object Above), press Command-Option-right bracket (]) (PC: Control-Alt-right bracket). In our example, we selected the top object (part of the face), and used the shortcut to select the next object below.

NEW STROKE OPTIONS IN ILLUSTRATOR CS2

This one is new and it may slip under your radar if you aren't looking closely at CS2's new feature list. In the Stroke palette, you'll see options for aligning a stroke. The default used to be center, which means that half of the stroke width would flow along the inside of the path and half would flow along the outside of the path. However, there was no way to change it. But now you can change this to outside or inside as well.

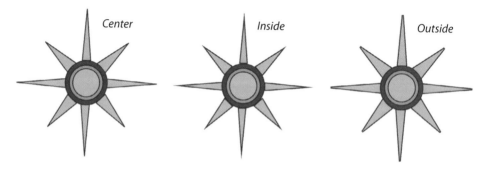

Center   Inside   Outside

SCALE STROKES & EFFECTS

When you scale an object to make it larger or smaller, you'll have to decide whether you want the stroke and effects to scale also (in general, this is usually the best choice). Although this option is controlled by the General Preferences (under the Illustrator menu in OS X or the Edit menu in Windows), there is a quicker way to change this setting. Double-click on the Scale tool to open its dialog. Either check or uncheck the Scale Strokes & Effects box, and that will not only change the setting for the selected object, but will also change the preference from then on.

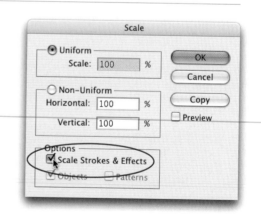

 **ODD NUMBERS**

You may find that you enter a value in the Transform palette and, after pressing Return (PC: Enter), you get an odd value. For example, you type in 3 for the width, but after pressing Return (PC: Enter), it says 3.01. One factor that can cause this is a function called Snap to Point. Turn this off from the View menu or press Command-Option-" (PC: Control-Alt-"), and you should now get the exact value you enter.

 **MOVE AND COPY**

To move an object to a specific area and copy it, use the Transform palette. Enter the amount you'd like to move the object in the X or Y field and press-and-hold the Option key (PC: Alt key) as you press Return (PC: Enter). Keep in mind the reference point in the proxy.

 ## STRAIGHT CUTS

Here's a weird one: The Knife tool (Shift-K) doesn't use the Shift key to cut in a straight line. Although every other tool uses Shift as a constraint for straight lines, with the Knife tool you hold down the Option key (PC: Alt key) to cut in a straight line. Use Option-Shift (PC: Alt-Shift) to cut in a straight horizontal or vertical line.

 ## MOVE IT BY MEASURE

The Move command (Object>Transform>Move) and the Measure tool (nested under the Eyedropper tool in the Toolbox) work very nicely together. Start by selecting your object, then click-and-drag with the Measure tool to "measure" the distance and angle you want to move the object. The numbers will appear in the Info palette (Window>Info), but more importantly, the Move command will use these measurements. Use the Move command (Command-Shift-M [PC: Control-Shift-M]) and click OK to move the object the specific distance and angle you just measured.

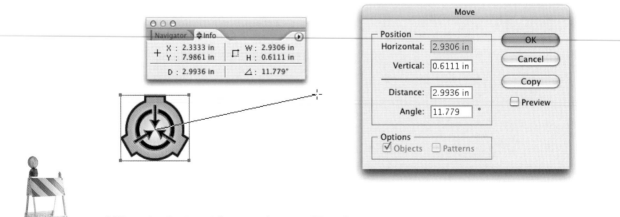

DRAW AND SMOOTH

When you're using the Pencil tool (N) and need to smooth out your path, just hold down the Option key (PC: Alt key) before clicking-and-dragging to temporarily activate and use the Smooth tool. Then let go of the key to return to the Pencil tool.

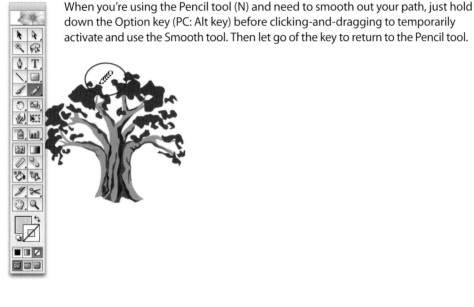

SIMPLIFY PATH

When you use the Simplify command (Object>Path>Simplify) to adjust a path, take advantage of the Show Original option to compare the effects of the Simplify command with the original path. The original path will be shown in red, while the simplified path will display in blue.

MAGIC WAND NOT WORKING

If the Magic Wand tool (Y) isn't doing its job the way you think it should (i.e., it's not selecting objects that it should be selecting), make sure the blending modes are not causing a problem. Double-click on the Magic Wand tool in the Toolbox to open its palette and uncheck Blending Mode. Why? When it is checked, the wand will only select objects with the same fill *and* the same blending mode. (*Note:* If this option isn't showing, go to the palette's flyout menu and select Show Transparency Options).

COPY WHILE TRANSFORMING

Selecting an object's bounding box while using the Selection tool (V) is a great way to make quick transformations, such as scaling and rotating without switching to the transformation tools. However, one thing it cannot do is to make a copy when rotating or scaling. To do this, you must use a transformation tool and hold down the Option key (PC: Alt key) as you rotate or scale.

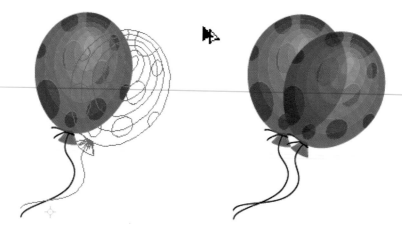

TRANSFORM AGAIN AND SEND TO BACK

An earlier tip told you not to do any additional operation after transforming an object or the Transform Again command wouldn't work. Well, here's one important exception to that rule. You can use the Arrange commands (such as Object>Arrange>Send to Back and Bring to Front) and still retain Transform Again. For example, you scale a circle by Option-clicking (PC: Alt-click-ing) on the object with the Scale tool (S) and pressing Copy to make a larger circle. By default, the larger circle will be in front, so use Object>Arrange>Send to Back to reposition the new circle. Then press Command-D (PC: Control-D) to Transform Again (copy and scale the larger circle), and then once again use the Object>Arrange>Send to Back command.

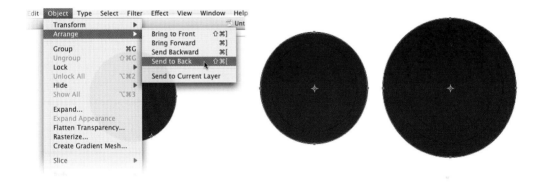

TRANSFORM AGAIN, AGAIN

You know that pressing Command-D (PC: Control-D) after transforming an object will apply the transformation again. However, did you know that you can do the same thing to an anchor point? Just select the Direct Selection tool (A) and move a single anchor point on the object. Here's the tip, though: You won't be able to press Command-D (PC: Control-D) to redo that transformation/move. You'll need to manually go through the Object menu under Transform>Transform Again to do this because pressing the Command key (PC: Control key) reverts the tool back to the Selection tool (V).

ALIGNING THE FAST WAY

A very common task in Illustrator is aligning objects horizontally and/or vertically. However, there's no keyboard shortcut for this task, and if you find yourself doing it a lot, then it can indeed become a nuisance. Well, don't let that stop you. Just record an action that does it for you. First, draw two objects on the artboard and select both of them. Then choose Window>Actions to display the Actions palette. Click the Create New Action button at the bottom of the palette, and be sure to assign a function key shortcut to it on the resulting dialog. Press Begin Recording, then align the Horizontal and Vertical centers of the two selected objects. Press the Stop Playing/Recording button at the bottom of the palette and you're done. Now just press the F-key shortcut you assigned to the action whenever you want to align selected objects.

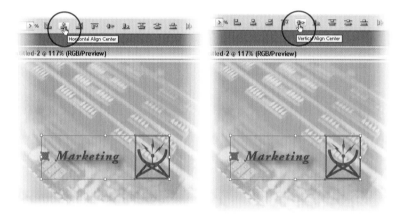

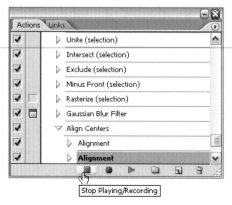

ALIGN TO A SPECIFIC OBJECT

The Align palette (Window>Align) is a simple way to take a number of selected objects and line them up vertically or horizontally by their edges or centers. You can control this alignment by lining up all objects with one specific object. To do this, select all the objects and then click on one object (all the objects will stay selected). Then click on the appropriate icon in the Align palette (or Control Palette) and all the objects will align relative to the object you clicked on. For example, we aligned all of the objects by selecting them and then clicking on the eye graphic. Then we clicked on the Horizontal Align Center icon in the Align palette.

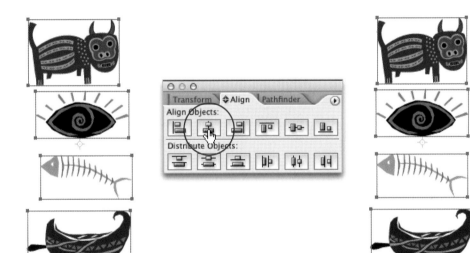

CONVERT DASHED STROKE TO OUTLINE

At first glance, it doesn't appear that it's possible to convert a dashed line to an outline. If you use either the Object>Expand or Object>Path>Outline Stroke command, you get a solid line. The solution? Select the path and from the Object menu choose Flatten Transparency. In the dialog, move the Raster/Vector Balance slider to 100, make sure Convert All Strokes to Outlines is checked, and click OK. You'll end up with an outlined dashed line (where each dash is a separate object).

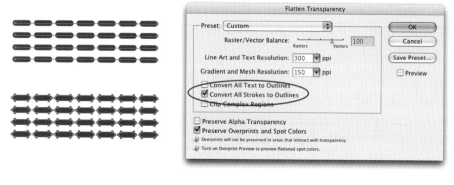

MAKE A MESH WITH TEXT

Here's a cool tip that comes courtesy of David Creamer in *Mac Design Magazine*. As an interesting way of transforming text without creating outlines, select the type with the Selection tool (V), and use the Object>Envelope Distort>Make with Mesh command (Command-Option-M [PC: Control-Alt-M]). The trick is to make the mesh have only one row and one column. Then use the Mesh tool (U) to distort the corner handles. To edit the text, select it again with the Selection tool, and go back to Object>Envelope Distort and choose Edit Contents (Command-Shift-V [PC: Control-Shift-V]).

 **DRAG-AND-DROP**

©BROOKE NUNEZ

Instead of copying-and-pasting from one document to another, just drag-and-drop. Select an object and use either selection tool to drag the object to a second open document. There's only one catch: If you drag from a document with objects on multiple layers, in the other document all objects will end up on one layer. To avoid this, use the Layers palette flyout menu, and choose Paste Remembers Layers—then the layers will be preserved when you select your object and drag-and-drop.

 THE MISSING TWIST TOOL

In Illustrator 10, there was a Twist tool (which was also named the Twirl tool in previous versions) nested under the Rotate tool, but it is not in CS2. Why? You'll have to ask Adobe that one, although we understand that it has to do with the inability of the Twist tool to twist things back to the way they were. Now if you want to twist an object, you'll have to use Effect>Distort & Transform>Twist. Although you have to distort numerically, the advantage of using the effect is that you can easily change the settings (by double-clicking on Twist in the object's Appearance palette [found under the Window menu]).

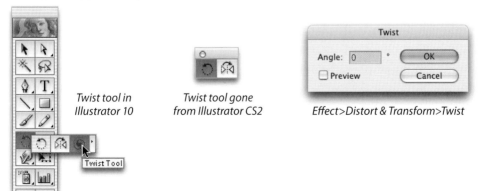

Twist tool in Illustrator 10

Twist tool gone from Illustrator CS2

Effect>Distort & Transform>Twist

Different Strokes

COLORS, SWATCHES, FILLS, AND STROKES

These are smokin' tips. Literally, they're

hoodlum tips, standing on the street

corner, smoking. Tips from the wrong side of

Different Strokes
colors, swatches, fills, and strokes

town, that could easily lead astray all the other

tips that are working so hard to stay on the

straight and narrow. Ever heard Illustrator users

talking about their preferences being corrupted

and having to delete them? Do you think that just

happens by accident? Oh no, my friend. Be very,

very careful. Don't get too close to these tricks or

your life may never be the same. We understand

the temptation—getting more work done in

less time, it's heady stuff. It may not seem like

much of anything at first. You record an action to

save yourself some time, but before you know it,

you're doing batch actions…and using keyboard

shortcuts like there's no tomorrow…and it all

starts from associating with those bandana-

wearing, rough-talking, good-for-nothing tips.

Hey, don't say we didn't warn you.

YOUR COLORS, EVERY TIME

You can customize the Swatches palette (Window>Swatches) to have your choice of colors, patterns, and gradients appear in every document. To do this, you need to open a document called Adobe Illustrator Startup, found in the Illustrator CS2 Applications (PC: Program Files) folder under Plug-ins. There are actually two documents, one for RGB and one for CMYK. Open the document that corresponds with whatever color schematic you use most often. Once the document is open, add or delete swatches for colors, gradients, and patterns. Save the document, restart Illustrator, and from then on, the Swatches palette will contain your swatches.

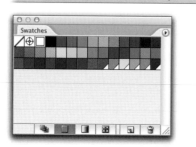

SLIGHTLY LIGHTER, SOMEWHAT DARKER

If you have created a color using CMYK or RGB sliders in the Color palette (Window>Color) and now you want a slightly lighter or darker version of that color, you can adjust all the sliders at the same time. Hold down the Shift key as you drag one slider and the other three sliders will move together, creating a lighter or darker shade of the color.

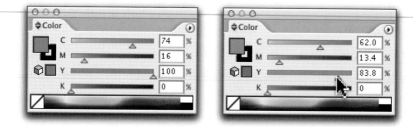

GRAB ONLY THE COLOR

©ISTOCKPHOTO/MARK STAY

By default, the Eyedropper picks up everything—fill and stroke color, stroke attributes, transparency, etc. (These options are set by double-clicking on the Eyedropper tool in the Toolbox.) To pick up only the color (without changing the default settings) press-and-hold the Shift key and click with the Eyedropper on an object that has the color you need.

MAKE YOUR OWN PATTERNS

Anything you drag into the Swatches palette (Window>Swatches) will become a pattern, but it takes a bit of planning to create a seamless repeating pattern. Start by creating a square with no stroke—pick a fill color if you want your pattern to have a background. Draw the shape you want in your pattern, center it, and then copy it four times, lining up each one's center on each corner of the square. Select the square, Copy it (Command-C [PC: Control-C]) and Paste in Back (Command-B [PC: Control-B]), and then change the fill to none. Select all the pieces (Command-A [PC: Control-A]) and drag them into the Swatches palette. Now you can use the pattern swatch to fill any object.

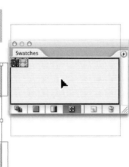

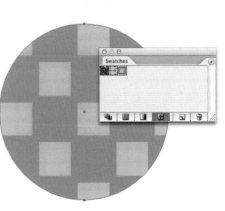

TRANSFORM JUST THE PATTERN

It's possible to transform only the pattern within an object, without moving the object itself. You can do this with any of the transformation tools (Rotate, Scale, Shear, etc.) while holding down the tilde (~) key. Keep the key held down as you transform—don't let go or the object will be transformed instead.

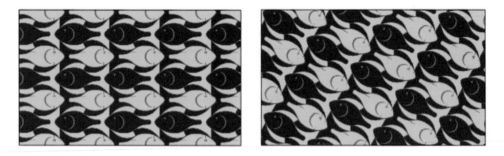

COLOR THE OPPOSITE

If you need to change the fill of an object and the stroke is active (or vice versa), the Color palette offers a simple solution. With the object selected, press-and-hold the Option key (PC: Alt key) as you click on the color ramp at the bottom of the Color palette, and the color will be applied to the opposite of what is active. That is, if the stroke is active, Option-click (PC: Alt-click) to apply the color to the fill. This only works when you click on the color ramp or the black or white squares to the right of the color ramp—it does not work in the Swatches palette.

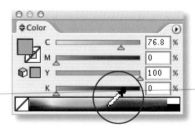

USE GLOBAL COLOR

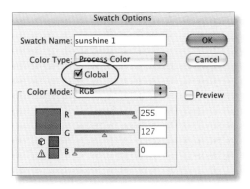

Global color lets you create a document in which you can easily change colors at once, throughout all objects. Start by creating a new swatch in the Swatches palette (Window>Swatches) by using the palette's flyout menu and choosing (strangely enough) New Swatch. Click on the Global checkbox. Use this color to fill and/or stroke images, using different percentages of the color (just make sure you have the color selected and then adjust the Tint percentage slider in the Color palette). You can also create a gradient using different percentages of the global color by dragging the swatch to the gradient ramp in the Gradient palette. Later, if you need to change all objects to a different color, you can either edit the global color by double-clicking it in the Swatches palette, or create a new global color swatch and press-and-hold the Option key (PC: Alt key) as you drag it over the original global color swatch. (Before replacing the global color, make a duplicate of the swatch by dragging it onto the New Swatch icon in the Swatches palette.)

BORROW SOME COLOR

You can grab colors (and more) from an existing Illustrator document without opening the file. From the Swatches palette (Window>Swatches), use the flyout menu and choose Open Swatch Library, then select Other Library. Then browse and find the document you want and click Open. A second Swatches palette will open with all the swatches from the other document. (One way to use this is to create for each client or project a document that contains only the swatches you use for that purpose, then load them as you need them.)

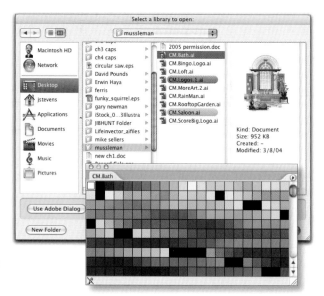

PERSISTENT SWATCHES

After you've loaded swatches from a preset library, you can make sure that library loads each time you launch Illustrator. To do that, first load the library from the Swatches palette's flyout menu. Once it's open, position the palette where you want it to appear, then use the flyout menu from that library's palette, and choose Persistent. (This also works for Symbols and Brushes libraries, but doesn't work on libraries that you've opened from another Illustrator document.)

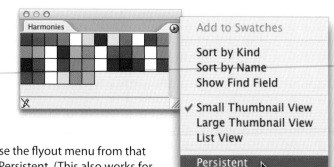

 **COLOR FROM ANYWHERE**

You can sample color from any-where on your computer—or anything you can see, that is. Just take the Eyedrop-per tool (I) and click-and-hold anywhere on the artboard. Then, while still holding, drag the Eyedrop-per tool over any color you can see, including in other applications, other files, or on your desktop. In this example, we're sampling a color from a photo that's open in Photoshop.

 GRADIENT PALETTE SHORTCUT

Here's a quick way to open the Gradient palette: Just double-click on the Gradient tool in the Toolbox and the palette will open (or move to the front if it's hidden behind other palettes).

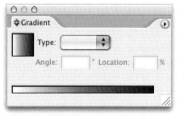

ONE-COLOR GRADIENT

To create a gradient using only one spot color, you'll get better printing results if you create a gradient that goes from 100% to 0% of the same color (rather than using white as the second color). Just drag your spot color twice to the Gradient Slider in the Gradient palette (found under the Window menu), then select the second color stop, go to the Color palette, and change its percentage to zero in the Tint Percentage field.

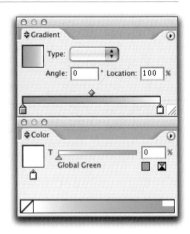

 COLOR STOP

You can pick a color from an object in a document and use it to color a gradient stop. In the Gradient Slider, click on the stop you want to change and then pick the Eyedropper tool. Hold down the Shift key and click on an object to use its fill color for the gradient stop.

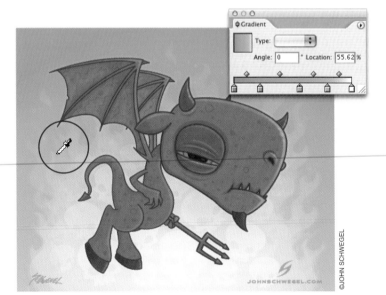

DUPLICATE A COLOR STOP

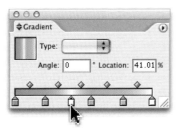

If you need to use the same color elsewhere in a gradient, you can easily copy a stop. In the Gradient Slider on the Gradient palette (Window>Gradient), press-and-hold the Option key (PC: Alt key), and then click on a stop and drag a copy to create a new color stop on the gradient.

SWAP STOPS

In the Gradient Slider on the Gradient palette (Window>Gradient), you can swap colors by holding down the Option key (PC: Alt key), and dragging an existing stop (the color you want) on top of another stop (the color you want to replace).

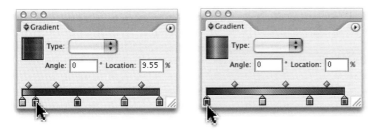

 **USE A SWATCH AS A STOP**

If you have selected an object filled with a gradient and you try to edit the gradient, you may run into a challenge. If you go to the Gradient palette (Window>Gradient), click on a color stop in the Gradient Slider, and then click on a swatch, the object's color will change to the swatch rather than editing the gradient. To apply a swatch to a color stop, click on the stop, hold down the Option key (PC: Alt key), and click on a swatch in the Swatches palette (Window>Swatches). You can also click-and-drag a swatch from the Swatches palette and drop it onto the Gradient Slider to create a new stop in that color (just don't let go of the swatch—click-and-drag in one step). If your stop changes color, but your gradient doesn't reflect the change, simply click on the stop and slide it a little. The gradient will then change.

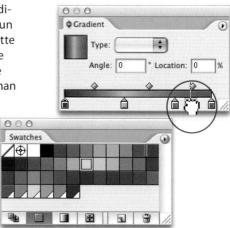

 **QUICK STROKE CHANGE**

Here's a great, quick way to change the stroke of a path, even if it's not selected. Just drag a swatch from the Swatches palette or Color palette (both found under the Window menu) onto an unselected path. If the stroke is not active in the Toolbox, press-and-hold the Shift key once you start to drag the swatch onto the path.

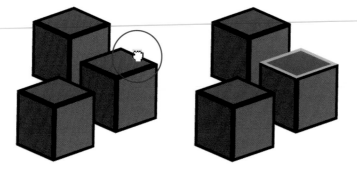

CHANGE COLOR MODES IN THE COLOR PALETTE

If you need to change the color mode being used by the Color palette (from RGB to CMYK, for example), just press-and-hold the Shift key, and click on the color ramp at the bottom of the palette. With each click, you'll cycle through the various color modes.

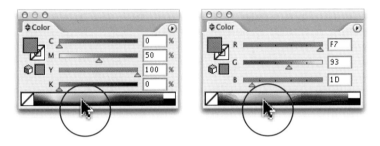

USE MULTIPLE STROKES IN APPEARANCE

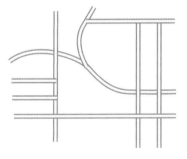

Here's a great way to use multiple strokes without creating multiple objects. Draw your path and in the Appearance palette (Window>Appearance), use the flyout menu to Add New Stroke. Double-click on each stroke in the Appearance palette and adjust the stroke width, color, and stacking order (using the Stroke palette, Color palette, etc.) to get the effect you want. (In our example, we chose a white, 5-point stroke and placed it above our wider 10-point stroke.) If you are working with multiple objects and need to get the "intersecting streets" look, select all the paths and press Command-8 (PC: Control-8) to create a compound path.

 **ROUND JOINS**

When you create a path that has a sharp corner, you have a couple of options for making it "less pointy" (how's that for technical terminology?). In the Stroke palette (found under the Window menu), you can either adjust the Miter Limit field by entering a lower number or, in many cases, it is simpler to change the join from Miter Join to Round Join or Bevel Join by clicking on one of the Join icons. (The same concept applies to the corners of a rectangle.) Remember to expand the Stroke palette (using the palette's flyout menu) if you can't see the Miter Limit or Join icons.

Default Miter Limit of 4 *Miter Limit of 1* *Round Join*

APPLY SAMPLED COLORS

After you've sampled a color from an object with the Eyedropper tool (I), you can apply the color to an unselected object by pressing-and-holding the Option key (PC: Alt key). This turns the Eyedropper tool into the Black-tipped Apply-it Eyedropper tool (okay, we made up that name)—click and the color is applied.

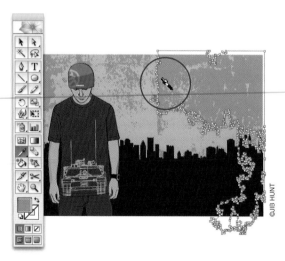

CHANGE LIVE PAINT BEHAVIOR

By default, the Live Paint Bucket (K) will paint only the fill of the area you've hovered over. (It paints with the Fill and Stroke colors showing in your Toolbox. To use the colors of another object, such as the small star in our image, click on that object and then Command-click [PC: Control-click] on the object you want to paint.) If you want to change the stroke color of an object using the Live Paint Bucket, press-and-hold the Shift key while hovering over the stroke and the cursor will change to a paintbrush, indicating you're now painting the stroke. (The other option is to double-click on the Live Paint Bucket and change the tool options to Paint Fills and Paint Strokes. Then the tool will affect either fill or stroke, depending on where it is positioned. You will see a paint bucket when you are hovering over the fill and a paintbrush when you are hovering over the stroke.)

SAME COLOR AGAIN

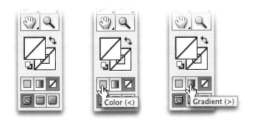

The Toolbox displays the last solid color and gradient fills you've used. After you have selected an object, check to see if your last-used color or gradient appears in the icons (shown here) just below the Fill and Stroke colors near the bottom of the Toolbox. If so, you can apply the last solid fill color you used by pressing the comma (,) key. To fill an object with the last gradient you used, press the period (.) key. Of course, this won't work if you're using the Type tool (T). (*Note:* Although Illustrator implies you should use the Shift key by showing < and > in the Toolbox, you don't need to do this. Instead, consider the keys as the comma and period keys.)

FILL AND STROKE FROM THE KEYBOARD

Before you choose a color, you need to indicate whether you are working on the fill or stroke for the selected object. At the bottom of the Toolbox, look at the two icons that represent the Fill (left) and Stroke (right). The icon in front indicates which is active, fill or stroke. If the stroke is active and you want to work on the fill (or vice versa), press X. Each time you press X, you will toggle between an active fill or stroke (unless you are using the Type tool).

Fill selected
after pressing X

Stroke selected
after pressing X

NONE IN A HURRY

Need to change the fill or stroke of an object to None? After indicating whether you want to affect the fill or the stroke (see previous tip), press the forward slash key (/). (If you need a reminder as to which slash key to use, look at the "None" symbol, as shown here. And if you're using the Type tool [T], stop it. It won't work for this tip.)

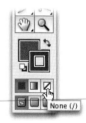

WANT THE OPPOSITE?

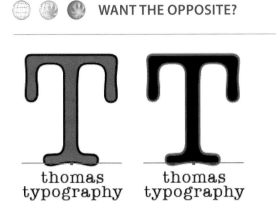

Okay, so you have an object that has a red fill and a black stroke and now you want to see it the other way around. Press Shift-X and the fill and stroke will be swapped (in this case resulting in a black fill and red stroke).

MAKE A SPOT COLOR

When you click on the New Swatch icon in the Swatches palette (Window>Swatches), you'll get, yes, a new swatch. However, the swatch will be a process color. If you want a spot color swatch, hold down the Command key (PC: Control key) as you click on the New Swatch icon. To edit your spot color, head to the Color palette (Window>Color).

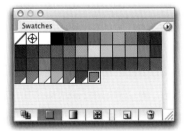

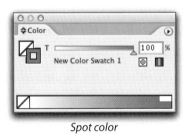

Spot color

Process color

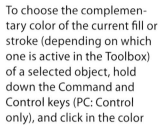 ## COMPLEMENTARY COLORS

To choose the complementary color of the current fill or stroke (depending on which one is active in the Toolbox) of a selected object, hold down the Command and Control keys (PC: Control only), and click in the color ramp at the bottom of the Color palette. (Or, use the flyout menu in the Color palette and choose Complement.)

 ## INVERT THE COLOR

To pick the inverse of the current fill or stroke (depending on which one is active in the Toolbox) of a selected object, press-and-hold Command-Shift (PC: Control-Shift), and click on the color ramp on the bottom of the Color palette. (Or, use the flyout menu in the Color palette and choose Invert.)

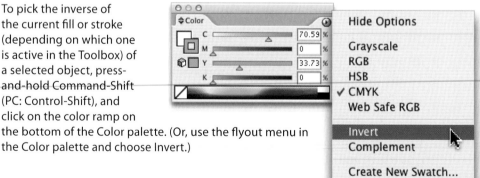

REPLACE ONE SWATCH WITH ANOTHER

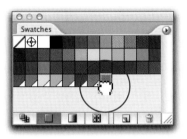

If you've used a color or gradient for various objects and you want to replace that color with another one, press-and-hold the Option key (PC: Alt key), and drag the new replacement swatch over the original swatch. If you're using global color, meaning you've checked Global in the New Swatch dialog when you created the color, all objects using the original global color will change to the new color. (*Note:* Doing this will remove the original swatch from the palette. So, if you want to keep the original color, drag the swatch onto the New Swatch icon to duplicate it before using this replacement method.)

GRAYSCALE OR COLOR GRAY

Huh? Okay, so you want to fill an object with 60% gray. You could change the Color palette (Window>Color) to Grayscale from the flyout menu and enter 60 in the Tint Percentage field. However, that means that your object will always be gray, so you won't be able to change it to color in the Color palette, unless you first change the mode of that object to CMYK. Instead, stick with CMYK and just enter 60 in the K field—that way you can always change to a color from the Color palette whenever you want.

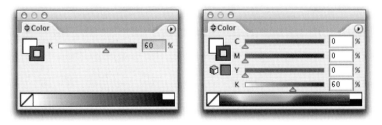

FIND A COLOR

If you need to pick a specific Pantone color, go to the Window menu and choose the appropriate Pantone library from the Swatch Libraries. Use the flyout menu in the Pantone palette and choose Show Find Field. Then enter the Pantone number you need in the Find field (type in only the number, there's no need for "Pantone").

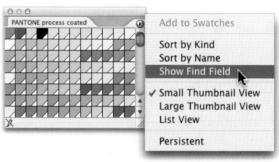

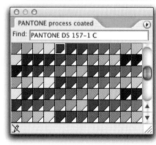

GRAYSCALE PRINT FROM A COLOR FILE

Although it is possible to print a grayscale version of a document using the Print command, on some color inkjet printers the results may be less than satisfactory. Instead, make a quick grayscale version of your document by selecting all the artwork and from the Filter menu, choosing

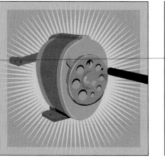

Colors>Convert to Grayscale (gradients and patterns will not be converted). If you like, save as a different name, or just print and then undo the filter.

SAVE SWATCH LIBRARIES

You can edit Illustrator's startup documents to customize your palettes, but this doesn't really help if you are constantly changing sets of swatches. Instead, consider saving and using libraries. Add and delete swatches until the Swatches palette contains your choice of swatches and then use the palette's flyout menu to choose Save Swatch Library. Name it and save it in the Swatches folder in the Illustrator CS2 Applications (PC: Program Files) folder under Presets. Restart Illustrator, and from then on you can access your library from the Window>Swatch Libraries>(yourlibrary).

 **EXPAND A GRADIENT**

There are times when you may
have to expand a gradient to
convert it to a series of objects
(for example, if you are having
trouble getting a gradient
to print and/or look the way
you want). With the object
selected, go to the Object
menu and choose Expand. In
the dialog, choose between
Gradient Mesh and Specify
Objects. To expand a gradi-
ent-filled object with the last-used settings, press-and-hold the Option key (PC: Alt key) as
you choose Object>Expand.

TEST PAGE

Considering how different shades of colors,
grays, and stroke widths can look on different
printers, you may want to create a printer test
page that contains boxes filled with a variety
of shades of gray, standard colors, paths with
different stroke widths, and type in various
small font sizes. Anytime you want to decide
on the best color, shade, or stroke width to
use, print your test page, and use that as your
guide. (If your final output is always the same
printer, create a test page that contains every
swatch and gradient and use it to choose
swatches based on the printed version rather
than the screen.)

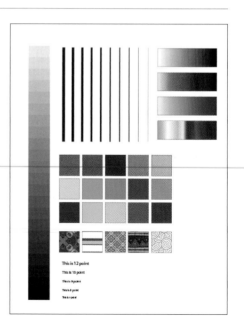

FADE TO NOTHING

Unfortunately, in Illustrator you cannot create a gradient that goes from a color to transparent as you can in Photoshop. To work around this, create a gradient using the color you need plus white. Fill the object with the gradient and then create an opacity mask to gradually change the object to transparent. To do this, create a rectangle slightly bigger than your object and position the rectangle over the object. Fill the rectangle with a black-to-white gradient, positioning the black over the area of the original object where you want the gradient to be see-through. Select both objects and from the Transparency palette (Window>Transparency), use the flyout menu to choose Make Opacity Mask. If you need to adjust the effect, click on the mask thumbnail (that's to the right of your object) in the Transparency palette and then adjust the position of the rectangle and/or the gradient. To return to regular editing, make sure you click on the object's thumbnail (that's to the left of the mask) in the Transparency palette.

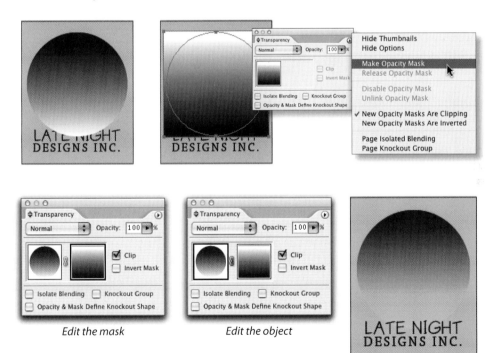

Edit the mask   Edit the object

 ## USE PREVIEW BOUNDS

By default, Illustrator uses the path of an object for measurements, alignments, etc., ignoring the stroke width. No matter how thick the stroke, the size of the object will be measured based on the position of the path. If you want to use the stroke width (and position) as the reference rather

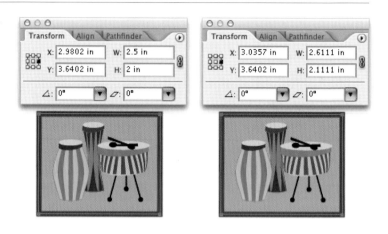

than the path, press Command-K (PC: Control-K) to go to the Preferences dialog and check Use Preview Bounds. From then on, all operations will be measured based on the thickness and position of the stroke, as shown here in the Transform palette (Window>Transform).

ONE-TIME PREVIEW BOUNDS

The only downside to the previous tip is that you change the setting for all operations to use the stroke width. If you're using the Align palette (Window>Align), there is a quicker way for one-time uses.

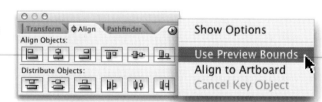

Use the flyout menu in the Align palette and click on Use Preview Bounds to turn it on when you want to use it and turn it off when you're done. In other words, the Align palette temporarily overrides the Preferences setting.

Okay, so this isn't really a chapter but more of a bonus section to the book. We thought it would be cool to show you what some

Sultans of Swing

a killer collection of illustrator artists

of the hottest artists out there are doing with Adobe Illustrator. These folks continually imagine new ways to combine the tools in Illustrator to create some stunning results. Plus, it's our way of thanking these folks who have allowed us to use their artwork in this book. We're continually amazed by the work that we see in this industry and we hope you enjoy the creative inspiration that we've added here.

Scott Hinton
scotthinton@bitwisesystems.com

David Pounds

davidpounds@hisnet.org

Philip J. Neal
www.pneal.com • Philip@3pixels.net

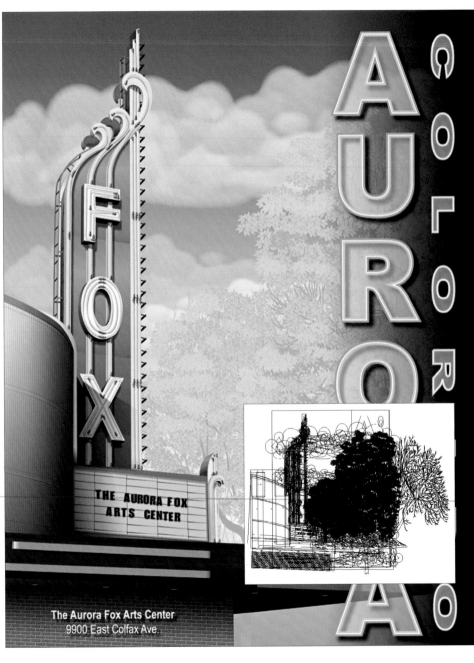

Mike Sellers
www.circlenlinestudios.com • mike@circlenlinestudios.com

Todd Ferris

www.warking.com • twf9999@optonline.net

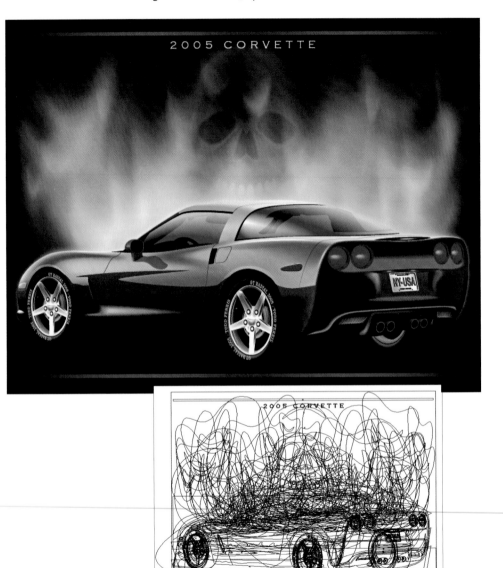

 ## Scott Weichert

www.weichertcreative.com • scott@weichertcreative.com

John Schwegel

www.johnschwegel.com • john@johnschwegel.com

Jib Hunt
www.jibhunt.com • jib@jibhunt.com

 **Brooke Nuñez**
www.lifeinvector.com • brooke@lifeinvector.com

Erwin Haya
www.onesickindividual.com • erwinhaya@hotmail.com

Mark Anderson
www.bigwhiskeyart.com

Christian Musselman

www.christianmusselman.com • chris@christianmusselman.com

Get Smart

LAYERS AND TRANSPARENCY

Imagine you have a stack of clear plastic sheets—you know, acetate. Each sheet has a colored graphic printed on it. Now imagine

Get Smart
layers and transparency

that you carefully overlay one sheet on top of another to create an informational graphic that shows a step-by-step procedure. With us so far? Okay, now imagine that you're standing beside an overhead projector (remember those?) with your stack of acetates, with your palms sweating, heart pounding, anxiously waiting for your presentation to start. Phew, we don't know about you, but that brings back nerve-wracking memories of the days before PowerPoint and data projectors. Makes working with Illustrator layers so easy that it's laughable. Ha ha ha… Ha!

 **DIM IMAGES**

A common approach to creating artwork in Illustrator is to import a photograph or a scanned image (File>Place) and to trace over it. You can make this procedure a little easier by putting the placed image on its own layer and then making it a template. Use the Layers palette's flyout menu to choose Template. The placed image will automatically be dimmed. To change the setting for the template, double-click on the layer

in the Layers palette to open the Layer Options dialog. In the Dim Images To field, enter a percentage. Then click on the Create New Layer icon at the bottom of the Layers palette and use your favorite creation tools to trace over the dimmed image.

 NAME THE NEW LAYER

When you add a new layer by clicking on the Create New Layer icon in the Layers palette (Window>Layers), the layer is automatically named "Layer x" (with x representing the next number). To create a new layer and name it, Option-click (PC: Alt-click) on the Create New Layer icon to open the Layer Options dialog where you can enter a name for the layer.

WHITE REALLY ISN'T WHITE

OK, maybe the title is exaggerated a bit. White is still white. But, the artboard in Illustrator isn't really white and will not reflect any transparency settings that white would normally influence. A little confused on what this means? Try this. Create an illustration or graphic in Illustrator—any small object should do—but just be sure it has no fill and a colored stroke, and you don't have anything in the layers below it. Select it, then in the Transparency palette (Window>Transparency), change the blend of that object to Soft Light. Nothing should happen. Now, add a rectangle with a white fill and no stroke to a layer below your object and you should see that top object disappear wherever it intersects with the white rectangle below it. This means that even though the artboard is white, it's not REALLY white.

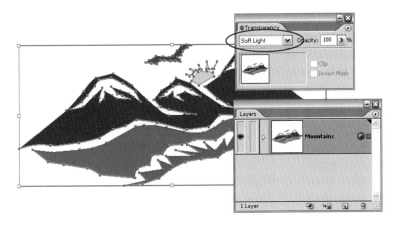

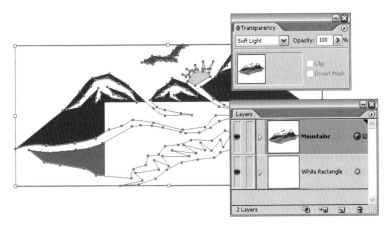

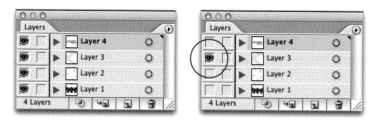 **HIDE OTHER LAYERS**

A quick way to view just one layer and hide all the rest of the layers is to press-and-hold the Option key (PC: Alt key) and click on the Eye icon beside the layer you want to view in the Layers palette. All the other layers will be hidden. Repeat to show all the layers again.

 **CHANGE ONE LAYER TO OUTLINE VIEW**

Changing to Outline view (Command-Y [PC: Control-Y]) is a great way see all the paths and anchor points. If you want to change only one layer to Outline view (rather than the entire document), press-and-hold the Command key (PC: Control key) and click on its Eye icon.

CHANGE OTHER LAYERS TO OUTLINE VIEW

When your artwork is in Outline view (Command-Y [PC: Control-Y]), things move faster since you're not waiting for the screen to redraw. Here's one way to take advantage of almost everything being in Outline view. Press-and-hold Command-Option (PC: Control-Alt) and click on the Eye icon beside the layer you need to change every other layer into Outline view, while your current layer remains in Preview view.

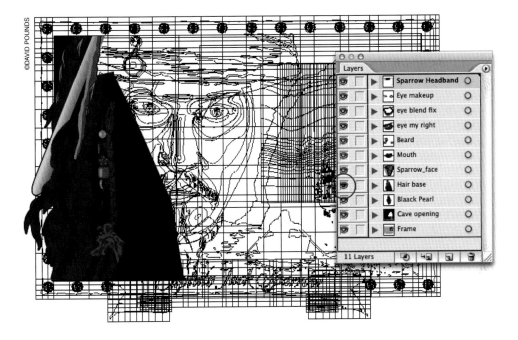

RELEASE THE LAYERS!

If you find your-
self creating Web
animations, then
Illustrator and its
Blend Tool (W)
can be your best
friend. How-
ever, when you
expand a Blend
in Illustrator
(Object>Blend>
Expand) it leaves
you with a Group.

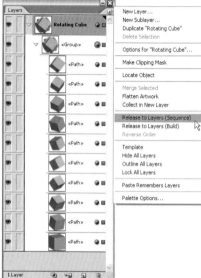

This makes it difficult to export to Photoshop
or ImageReady for animation since exporting to PSD will flatten the Group layer. To get
around this, immediately after Expanding the
Blend, choose Release to Layers (Sequence)
from the Layers palette's flyout menu. This
will convert all of the paths in the group to
layers, thus preserving each object when you
export to a PSD file.

COPY AN OBJECT TO A LAYER

To move a selected object onto a different layer, look
for the tiny square to the far right of the current layer's
name in the Layers palette. Drag that square to a different layer and the object will move to that layer. However, if you want to copy the object so that it stays on
its current layer and a copy appears on a different layer,
hold down the Option key (PC: Alt key) as you drag the
small square.

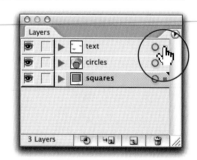

DUPLICATE THE ENTIRE LAYER

To quickly make an exact duplicate of a layer—and therefore, of all the objects on that layer—click on the layer name, then press-and-hold the Option key (PC: Alt key) as you drag that layer onto the Create New Layer icon at the bottom of the Layers palette.

 SELECT EVERYTHING ON A LAYER

How many times have you wanted to select every single object on a layer? Of course, the Select>All command won't help since every object on every layer would be selected. Here's the solution: In the Layers palette, locate the layer whose objects you want to select and either click on the small box (or empty space) to the right of the round button to the far right of the layer name, or Option-click (PC: Alt-click) on the name of the layer. All the objects on that layer will be selected.

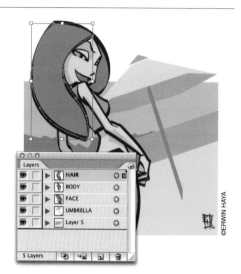

©ERWIN HAYA

 SELECT EVERYTHING ON MULTIPLE LAYERS

To take the previous tip a step further, if you need to select all of the objects on multiple layers, Option-Shift-click (PC: Alt-Shift-click) on the names of the contiguous layers whose objects you need to select, or Command-Option-click (PC: Control-Alt-click) to select non-contiguous layers.

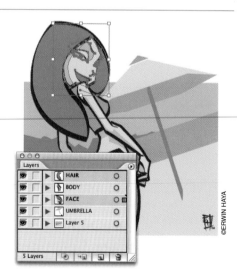

©ERWIN HAYA

LOCK ALL OTHER LAYERS

Locking objects is a very effective way to work—you can still see the objects but you cannot select or alter them by mistake. To lock every layer except the one you're working on, Option-click (PC: Alt-click) on the empty box next to the Eye icon on your current layer. All the layers, except the one you're working on, will be locked. Repeat the same operation to unlock all the layers.

©TODD FERRIS/POSE BY STEVE FERRIS

 USE LAYERS TO UNLOCK INDIVIDUAL OBJECTS

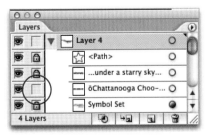

For many people, the first shortcuts they memorize are used to lock and unlock objects. Unfortunately, Command-2 (PC: Control-2) will lock one object, while Command-Option-2 (PC: Control-Alt-2) will unlock all objects. Sadly, there is no keyboard command to unlock just the last object that you locked a moment ago. The Layers palette offers a great alternative: Expand the layer by clicking on the triangle beside the layer's name, and then click the Lock icon to the left of the individual sublayer (object) you need to work with. (This only works if sublayers are locked, rather than the entire layer being locked.)

LOCATE LAYER

If you need to figure out what layer or sublayer an object is on, try this method. Click on the object to select it and then from the Layers palette's flyout menu, choose Locate Object. The sublayers will be expanded to reveal the location of the selected object.

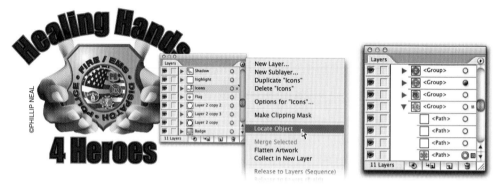

JUMP TO A LAYER

Here's a Windows-only tip that lets you jump to a specific layer in a long list in your Layers palette. Press-and-hold Control-Alt and click in the Layers palette. A solid black line will appear around the interior of the palette. Start typing the layer name to jump to that layer. (If you have a bunch of layers called "Layer 1," "Layer 2," and so on, just type the number and you'll jump to that layer.)

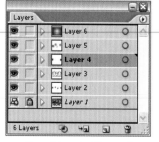

Layers palette selected   *Type 4 to select Layer 4*

CUSTOM LAYER ROW SIZE

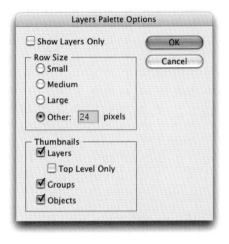

In the Palette Options dialog (found using the Layers palette flyout menu), you can choose between small, medium, and large row sizes. But, in addition to picking between those built-in sizes, you can make your own by choosing Other and entering a specific size. This is another one of these tips that you may not use often, but there are times when it's a perfect solution for those Goldilocks situations (this one is too small, this one is too big, but this one is just right).

EXPAND ALL SUBLAYERS

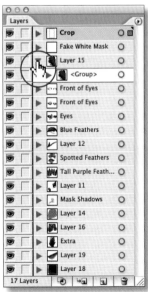

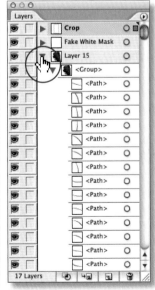

To see all the sublayers in the Layers palette, Option-click (PC: Alt-click) on the expansion triangle beside one of the layers. All the layers will be expanded to display all of their sublayers. (*Note:* This works differently depending on what sublayers you already have expanded.)

Layer expanded without Option-clicking

Layer expanded by Option-clicking

 **NEW LAYER ON TOP**

When you click on the Create New Layer icon in the Layers palette, the new layer is created right above the current layer. If you want the new layer to be added at the very top of all the layers, hold down the Command key (PC: Control key) as you click on the Create New Layer icon.

 **NEW LAYER BELOW**

If you want a new layer to be created below the current layer, Command-Option-click (PC: Control-Alt-click) on the Create New Layer icon. The Layer Options dialog will open, but once you click OK, the new layer will be created immediately below the current layer (here we've added a new layer named "additional text" below the layer named "balls").

TARGET A LAYER

The empty circle to the right of a layer name serves a very important purpose: When you click on the circle, you are targeting the entire layer. Change the layer's appearance and every object on that layer will have the same appearance. For instance, this applies if you have the layer targeted and then select options in the Appearance and Graphic Styles palettes or use options from the Effect menu, such as Brush Strokes. Once a layer has been targeted and a new appearance applied, the empty circle changes to a shaded circle.

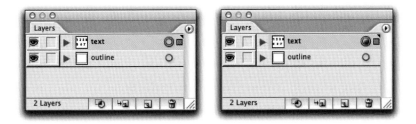

MOVING TARGETS

If you have targeted a layer and have changed its appearance, you can easily change your mind and apply the appearance to a different layer. Just click on the shaded circle and drag it onto an empty circle beside a different layer. The look will be moved from the original layer and applied to the other layer.

MOVING TARGETS, PART TWO

Here's another possibility: You love the look of one targeted layer so much that you also want to apply that look to another layer. Instead of moving the target, copy it by pressing-and-holding the Option key (PC: Alt key) as you drag the target from the current layer to another layer (note the plus sign beside your pointer).

PASTE REMEMBERS LAYERS

This command is very important when copying-and-pasting objects between documents. It is also an important option when copying-and-pasting in the same document. By default this option is turned off, so when you first start working with layers, you may want to go to the Layers palette's flyout menu and select Paste Remembers Layers. Then it will stay on, even when you create new documents.

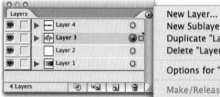

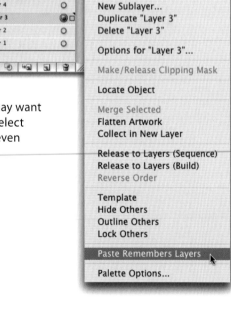

MIRROR REFLECTIONS

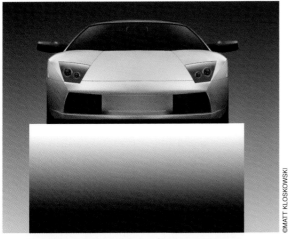

©MATT KLOSKOWSKI

Want to create a mirror reflection right inside Illustrator? It's easy. First you'll need to duplicate whatever object you want to create the mirror reflection of so you have two of them. Next, select the object and choose Object>Transform>Reflect. Pick the horizontal option and click OK. Position the duplicate toward the bottom of the original. Next, click the Create New Layer icon at the bottom of the Layers palette to get a blank layer above the layer with your objects. On the new layer, create a rectangle that covers the duplicate object, fill it with a white to black linear gradient, and set the stroke to none. Select both the rectangle and the duplicate object and choose Make Opacity Mask from the Transparency palette's flyout menu. Instant reflection!

 **LAYER COMPS?**

Photoshop CS2 has a great feature called Layer Comps, which helps you save different layer combinations in one document. Although Illustrator CS2 doesn't have the same feature, you can create a similar effect using custom views. Hide one or more layers by clicking on the Eye icons in the Layers palette, and then from the View menu, create a New View, give it a name in the dialog, and click OK. Repeat this to create as many different combinations of layers as you want and then choose your named views from the View menu to look at the different combinations. (*Note:* Custom views work best with top-level layers rather than sublayers.) If you want, you can even add a keyboard shortcut to these "layer comps" using Edit>Keyboard Shortcuts to assign a shortcut to Custom View 1, Custom View 2, etc.

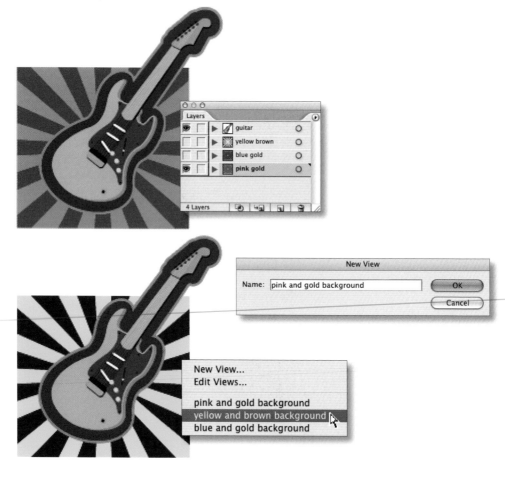

SELECTING MULTIPLE LAYERS

Hold down the Shift key to select more than one layer in the Layers palette (how's that for a staggeringly surprising tip?). Only problem is, you can only select contiguous layers that way (meaning layers that are above or below one another). To select multiple layers anywhere in the list of layers, hold down the Command key (PC: Control key) and click to select non-contiguous layers.

©DAVID POUNDS

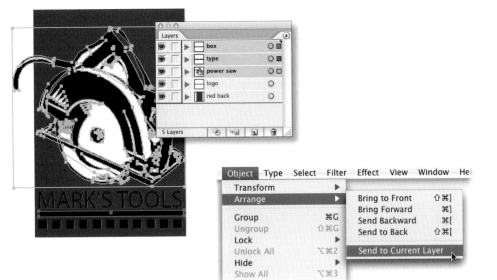

MOVE OBJECTS TO A DIFFERENT LAYER

As we saw earlier, you move a selected object to a different layer by clicking on the small square and dragging it to a different layer. However, this won't work if you need to move a bunch of objects from various layers to one layer. To do this, you'll have to use the Selection tool (V) and Shift-click to select the objects you need to move and then click on the name of the layer that you want to move them to. Then from the Object menu choose Arrange>Send to Current Layer.

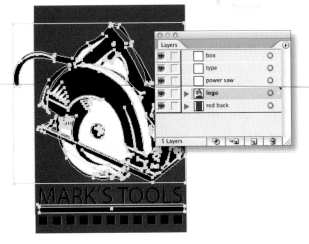

VECTOR TEMPLATES?

Typically, a placed raster image is used as a template to create an illustration. After placing the image (File>Place), choose Template from the Layers palette's flyout menu and if you want, use the Layers Options dialog to further dim the template for easier tracing. Just double-click on your layer name and in the dialog, click the Template checkbox. The Dim Images To field will be editable and you can enter a percentage. But, can you use an Illustrator (vector) object as a template? Well, yes and no. While you can turn a vector layer into a template using the same method just described, you cannot dim an Illustrator object. Another option would be to rasterize the object and then turn it into a template. Choose File>Place to get the vector image, and from the Object menu choose Rasterize. Then use the Layers palette's flyout menu to make the rasterized object into a template. You know the layer is a template when the Template icon appears in the Eye icon box to the left of the layer name. (*Note:* You may want to duplicate the original object before rasterizing just so you have a backup plan.)

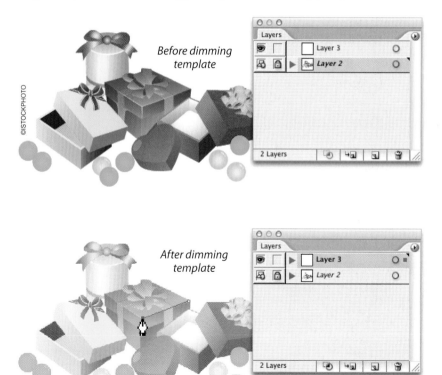

Before dimming template

©ISTOCKPHOTO

After dimming template

DON'T PRINT

Here's a simple way to tell at a quick glance if the Print option is turned off in the Layer Options dialog, meaning this layer won't print: Just look at the name of the layer. If the layer name appears in italics, the option to print has been turned off. Double-click on the layer name to open the Layer Options dialog and turn on printing by clicking the Print checkbox (and the display of the layer name will return to standard type).

NO SUBLAYERS

To simplify the display of the Layers palette, use the flyout menu to choose Palette Options. In the dialog, check the Show Layers Only box to hide everything except the top-level layers.

HIDE TEMPLATE

View	Window	Help
Outline		⌘Y
Overprint Preview		⌥⇧⌘Y
Pixel Preview		⌥⌘Y
Proof Setup		▶
Proof Colors		
Zoom In		⌘+
Zoom Out		⌘−
Fit in Window		⌘0
Actual Size		⌘1
Hide Edges		⌘H
Hide Artboard		
Show Page Tiling		
Show Slices		
Lock Slices		
Hide Template		⇧⌘W
Show Rulers		⌘R
Hide Bounding Box		⇧⌘B
Show Transparency Grid		⇧⌘D

If you've used a template in your document, you can quickly toggle the template on and off (showing and hiding the template) by pressing Command-Shift-W (PC: Control-Shift-W). This command can also be found under the View menu, as shown here.

WHEN SELECT ALL DOESN'T WORK

Object	Type	Select	Filter
Transform			▶
Arrange			▶
Group			⌘G
Ungroup			⇧⌘G
Lock			▶
Unlock All			⌥⌘2
Hide			▶
Show All			⌥⌘3
Expand...			

Object	Type	Select	Filter
Transform			▶
Arrange			▶
Group			⌘G
Ungroup			⇧⌘G
Lock			▶
Unlock All			⌥⌘2
Hide			▶
Show All			⌥⌘3
Expand...			

If you use Command-A (PC: Control-A) to Select All, it may not actually select *all* of your artwork. If you have locked or hidden objects on layers or sublayers, objects on those layers will not be selected. To make sure that Select All will really select everything, use the Unlock All and Show All commands (from the Object menu), then use the Select All command.

CHAPTER 7 • Layers and Transparency   **175**

 **MERGE SELECTED**

If your Layers palette is getting a little out of hand with way too many layers, there's a simple solution. After selecting the layers you want (see previous tip), use the Layers palette's flyout menu to choose Merge Selected and turn those separate layers into one layer with sublayers. For example, if you select three layers, each with two sublayers, and use Merge Selected, you will get one layer made up of six sublayers. The merged layer will use the name of the last layer you select.

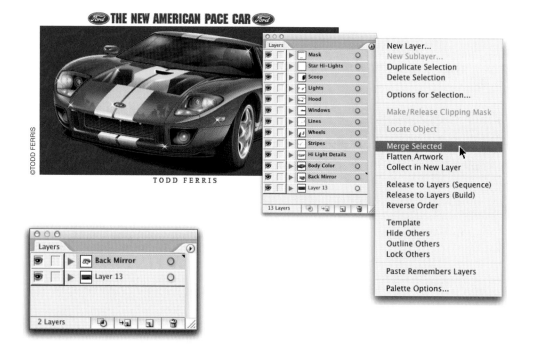

TODD FERRIS

COLLECT IN A NEW LAYER

As we saw in the previous tip, the Merge Selected command in the Layers palette turns selected layers and sublayers into a new layer with sublayers. If you want to preserve the structure of layers and sublayers, select the layers and from the Layers palette's flyout menu, choose Collect in New Layer. A brand new layer will be created that contains the layers and sublayers from the selected layers. (I just said "layer" 14…no, 15 times, but who's counting?)

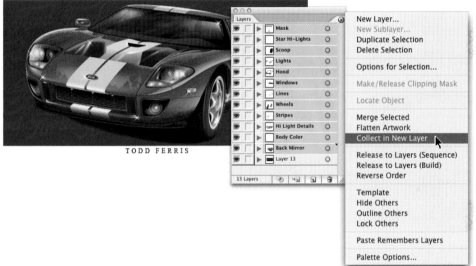

TODD FERRIS

Extreme Makeover

SYMBOLS, BRUSHES, APPEARANCE, FILTERS, AND EFFECTS

Just for fun, we thought we'd present

this entire chapter in a Jeopardy *format.*

You know, answers in the form of questions?

Extreme Makeover
symbols, brushes, appearance, filters, and effects

Think about it—it would be great: "I'll take the

Appearance palette for $500 please, Alex." "It will

ensure that all new artwork doesn't take on the

appearance of the previously created artwork."

"What is the New Art Has Basic Appearance

icon?" Ding ding ding ding! Wouldn't that be

great? There'd be no other chapter like it! Why do

we get the feeling that you're not with us on this

one? Okay, okay, how about this: "Name the top

reason for creating your own symbol?" Survey

says… Wait, don't turn the page, we've got more

game show ideas for this chapter…

WHAT IS NEW ART HAS BASIC APPEARANCE?

One important part of the Appearance palette (Window>
Appearance) is the New Art Has Basic Appearance icon. It's
on by default, which means that every time you create a
new object, that object will use the "basic" fill and stroke.
What's the basic appearance? The last fill and stroke you've
used for that object. However, click on the icon to turn it
off if you have created a specific appearance (using styles,
effects, etc.) and want to create a whole series of new
objects with the same look. In effect, when the icon is on,
all new objects will use the basic fill and stroke for that
particular object. When the icon is off, all new objects will
use the last appearance (including styles, effects, etc.) you
created for any object.

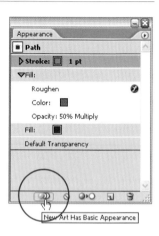

EFFECT GALLERY

Here's a huge speed tip when working with various effects in Illustrator CS2. Choose Effect>
Effect Gallery. Your first thought is probably, "What the heck is this?!" Rightfully so, since Adobe
really didn't make a big deal out of this one and nobody is talking about it. However, it's a huge
time saver because you can preview various effects all within one dialog instead of looking at
each effect, canceling out of the dialog, and going through the Effect menu all over again to
preview another effect.

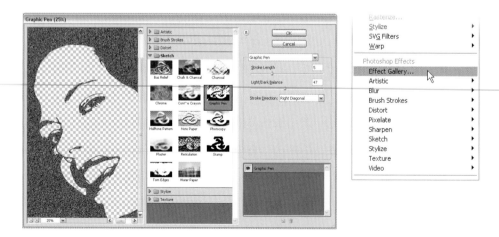

SCRUBBY SLIDERS

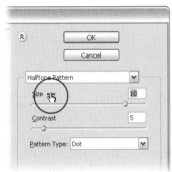

You may first be asking, "What the heck is a scrubby slider?" A scrubby slider is a newer way to adjust settings in dialogs and palettes without using the keyboard. To see what we mean try this: Apply a Halftone Pattern effect to an object in Illustrator (Effect>Sketch>Halftone Pattern). When the dialog opens, position your cursor over the word Size in the settings on the right. Note the little arrows that appear as the cursor. This is a scrubby slider. You can move your mouse to the left or to the right to adjust the setting without ever touching your keyboard. Note that not all settings in Illustrator have been updated with this ability.

CREATING ARROWHEAD DESIGNS

Did you know that you can add an arrowhead to a selected path using Filter>Stylize>Add Arrowheads? No? Well then, that's a bonus tip just for you. Just click on the arrows below the Start and End options to select your arrowheads' style. If you did know that already, then here's your tip: After using the Add Arrowheads filter, use the Direct Selection tool (A) to select the path. Then delete the path (keeping just the arrowhead), and you've got another source for simple shapes that you can use in your artwork.

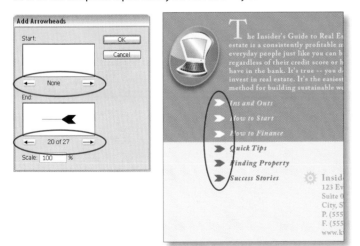

SYMBOLISM CHOOSER

Here's a cool way (thanks to Mordy Golding, former Adobe Illustrator Product Manager) to switch Symbolism tools on the fly, without using the Toolbox. Just press Control-Option as you click-and-hold (PC: Alt-Right-click-and-hold) with the Symbolism tool you're using, and all the Symbolism tools will appear in a circle. Move toward the tool you want until the cursor changes, release, and start using the new tool.

USING THE EYEDROPPER TO SAMPLE APPEARANCE

Click on an object with the Eyedropper tool (I) to sample its appearance and then press-and-hold the Option key (PC: Alt key) while using the Eyedropper tool to apply that appearance to another object. Okay, so you probably knew that already. One of the Eyedropper tool's hidden talents is to sample the appearance from multiple objects. (Before you try this, double-click the Eyedropper tool in the Toolbox to make sure that the Appearance options are selected.) With no objects selected in your document, use the Eyedropper tool to select your first color, then press Option-Shift (PC: Alt-Shift) and click on a second object to get your next color. Press-and-hold the Option key (PC: Alt key) and click on an object to apply both (or all) the sampled appearances to that object. If you're not totally satisfied with the result, you can change the order of the various fills and strokes in the Appearance palette.

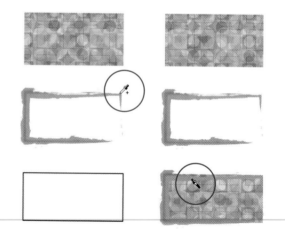

DRAG AN APPEARANCE

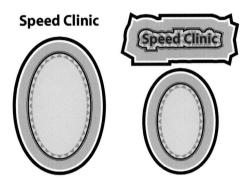

Speed Clinic

If you have created an appearance and want to apply the same look to a different object, here's a simple solution. Select the object whose appearance you want to use (in our example, we used an outlined blue and green oval) and click-and-drag its small preview thumbnail from the Appearance palette onto the other object(s) on the artboard (in our example, we dragged it onto the words Speed Clinic). If you don't see the preview, choose Show Thumbnail from the Appearance palette's flyout menu.

MERGE STYLES

If all the built-in graphic styles aren't enough for you, you can create additional styles by merging existing styles together. Find two (or more) styles you like in the Graphic Styles palette (Window>Graphic Styles) and select them. If the styles are adjacent in the Graphic Styles palette, you can press the Shift key and click on them; otherwise, you'll have to Command-click (PC: Control-click) on the styles. Then from the flyout menu, choose Merge Graphic Styles. A dialog will ask you to name the new style that your selected styles will create.

INSTANT LICHTENSTEIN OR POP ART DOT EFFECT

Bet you didn't think you'd get an art history lesson here, did you? Well Roy Lichtenstein (October 27, 1923–September 29, 1997) was a prominent American pop artist whose work borrowed heavily from popular advertising and comic book styles. His illustrations often contained areas of solid color with other areas of dots. You can recreate this style in Illustrator easily. Start out with an illustration and pick a surface that you'd like to add the dot effect to. Duplicate that layer or sublayer by dragging it onto the Create New Layer icon at the bottom of the Layers palette (Window>Layer), so you have two copies (in this example, we've duplicated the layer with the face on it). Next, on the flyout menu in the Swatches palette, select Open Swatch Library>Other Swatch Library. Navigate to the Presets>Patterns>Basic Graphics folder and choose the Basic_Graphics_Dots.ai file. Click on one of the dots patterns to apply it (we used the 10 dpi 40% pattern). Lock all other layers and sublayers except the one that now has the dots on it by Option-clicking (PC: Alt-clicking) in the empty box to the left of the dot layer (to the right of the Eye icon) in the Layers palette. Then go to the Object menu and choose Expand. Deselect everything (Command-Shift-A [PC: Control-Shift-A]). Use the Direct Selection tool (A) to select a single dot, and from the Select menu, choose Same>Fill Color. Choose a color that is slightly darker than your fill color on the surface you duplicated. Deselect everything again and watch your illustration turn into a Lichtenstein!

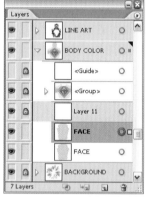

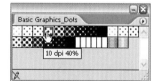

APPLY THE SAME EFFECT AGAIN

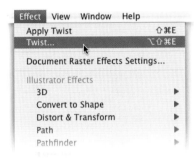

To reapply the last Effect menu command you used with exactly the same settings, press Command-Shift-E (PC: Control-Shift-E). To apply the same effect but change the settings, press Command-Option-Shift-E (PC: Control-Alt-Shift-E) to open a dialog for the effect.

FILTERS VS. EFFECTS? WHAT'S THE DIFFERENCE?

The difference between a filter and an effect is what Illustrator does to the object you apply it to. For example, draw a simple shape on the artboard. Duplicate it so the two are next to each other. Select the first shape and choose Filter>Distort>Twist and change the Angle setting to 150°. Then select the second shape and choose Effect>Distort & Transform>Twist and use the same 150° setting. They should both look identical at this point. But, if you choose View>Outlines, notice how the shape with the Filter applied to it has changed while the other one has not. This is because filters change the underlying structure of any paths they're applied to, while effects only change the appearance. The most important point to glean from this tip is that a filter is permanent and an effect is "live". This means that you can go back and change the settings of the effect (or remove it altogether) at any time.

RESET EFFECT AND FILTER SETTINGS

In many of Illustrator's Effect and Filter menu options, you can "start over" without closing the dialog that appears by pressing the Option key (PC: Alt key). The Cancel button will change to Reset—click Reset to revert all the settings to their default. For instance, we selected an object and chose Effect>Artistic>Dry Brush. After we changed a few of the settings, we decided to revert to the default settings using this tip. To find out which effects or filters dialogs this works in, try it!

ADD A SECOND STROKE

Unfortunately, you cannot apply a filter or an effect to just the stroke of an object. You could draw the stroke separately, but then you'd have to worry about grouping the two objects. Instead, with the object selected, use the flyout menu in the Appearance palette (Window>Appearance) to choose Add New Stroke. Click on the new stroke to highlight it in the Appearance palette, change its color using either the Color palette or the Swatches palette, and change its Weight by going to Window>Stroke. Then go the Effect menu and pick an effect. That way, if you change the size of the original object, this second stroke will automatically change, too.

 **DROP SHADOWS**

Here's a great tip for getting a better drop shadow effect in Illustrator. While you can control the offset, opacity, and blur settings of a drop shadow, there's really no way to control the thickness. If you try to do this by changing the offset value too much, it'll just make the drop shadow separate from the overlying object and appear to be raised higher. Instead, try this: Create some type and choose Effect>Stylize>Drop Shadow. Use the following settings:

> Mode: Normal
> Opacity: 100%
> X Offset: 2 pt
> Y Offset: 2 pt
> Blur: 0 pt
> Color: Black

It looks nice, but the effect is too thin. To make it thicker, go to the Appearance palette (Window>Appearance), and just duplicate the Drop Shadow item a few times. Each time you duplicate it the drop shadow effect will get thicker.

CHECK DOCUMENT RASTER EFFECTS SETTINGS

Before you start applying all kinds of raster effects or filters, make sure you have chosen the optimal raster quality settings for your document. From the Effect menu, choose Document Raster Effects Settings. In the dialog, choose the resolution, background (white or transparent), and options for anti-alias and clipping masks. These settings are document-wide, affecting all raster filters and effects. By default, the resolution is set to 72 ppi, so make this decision early on. If you change the resolution after creating objects and applying effects, the new resolution setting will be applied and the effects can change. For example, we had applied the Halftone Pattern effect to a logo, but the effect was changed after we altered the Document Raster Effects Settings.

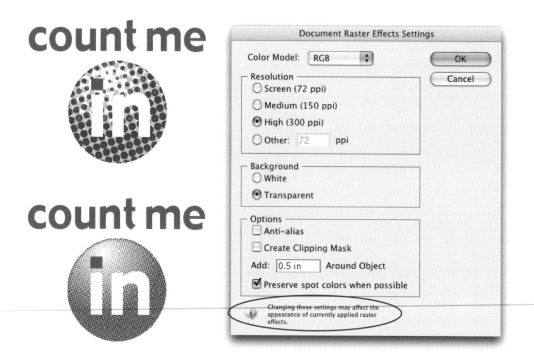

BREAKING A LINK TO A STYLE

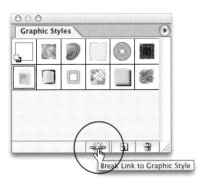

If you have applied a graphic style to a number of objects and later redefine the style in the Appearance palette (Window>Appearance), all the objects will update to the new style (they do not have to be selected). You can also ensure one object does not change from the original style by breaking the link to the style. Select the one object you don't want to change and click on the broken chain icon at the bottom of the Graphic Styles palette (Window> Graphic Styles). Now, if you change the settings for the graphic style in the Appearance palette and choose Redefine Graphic Style from the Appearance palette's flyout menu, the unlinked graphic will not change. There is no re-link icon, so you'll have to reapply the graphic style by selecting the object and clicking on the style in the Graphic Styles palette.

DISAPPEARING EFFECTS WHEN SWITCHING BETWEEN RGB AND CMYK

Some Effect menu options, such as the Artistic set, only work in RGB mode. This means if you change the Document Color Mode to CMYK in the File menu, the effect cannot be preserved (in other words, the effect you applied to an object will disappear, as it did here in our example using Effect>Brush Strokes>Spatter). To avoid this, before changing to CMYK mode, from the Object menu choose Expand Appearance (keeping in mind that your object will be converted to an image that cannot be edited to the same degree as when you started).

Object with Spatter effect   *Effect removed in CMYK mode*

ADD STROKE TO PLACED IMAGE OR PHOTO

If you want to add a stroke to a placed image (File>Place) you can, but it's not as simple as choosing a color for the stroke. You could draw a rectangle the same size, but there's an easier way. With the placed image selected, go to the Appearance palette (Window>Appearance) and choose Add New Stroke from the flyout menu. Then from the Effect menu choose Path>Outline Object. Change the stroke color and weight, and you're all set.

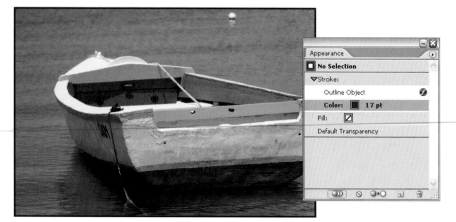

 **REDEFINE SYMBOLS**

If you have created and used a symbol in your document, you can easily change all instances by redefining the symbol. Place an instance of your symbol from the Symbols palette and use the Object>Expand command to edit the original artwork. Make the changes to the artwork and keep it selected. In the Symbols palette, click once on the original symbol, and from the palette's flyout menu, choose Redefine Symbol. All instances will automatically change to the edited symbol.

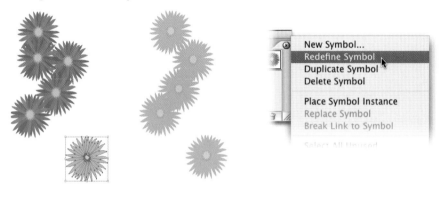

 VIEWING THE INTENSITY OF THE SYMBOL TOOLS

To find out the Intensity setting for the Symbolism tools, you could double-click on the active Symbolism tool in the Toolbox (say, for instance, the Symbol Stainer tool). But, for a quick visual clue, check out the brush's outline color. If it's very light gray, the tool has a low Intensity setting; if the brush outline is dark, the Intensity setting is high. Okay, so it's not an incredibly accurate measurement, but it will tell you very quickly if you need to change the setting.

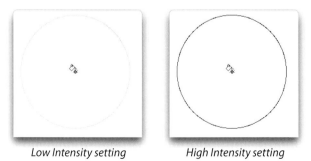

Low Intensity setting   *High Intensity setting*

MORE INTENSITY, DIFFERENT SIZE

When you are using any of the Symbolism tools, you can use these keyboard shortcuts: Press Shift-right bracket (]) to increase the brush intensity (the rate of change) or Shift-left bracket ([) to decrease the intensity. Press the bracket keys alone to change the brush size: left bracket to make the brush smaller or right bracket to make the brush bigger.

Lower Intensity setting

Increased Intensity setting

CHANGE MULTIPLE SYMBOLS

By default, the Symbolism tools will affect whatever symbol is selected in the Symbols palette (Window>Symbols). So, if you have multiple symbols on the artboard, only the selected symbol will be affected by the Symbolism tools. The Symbolism tools can influence multiple symbols at the same time: Just Shift-click in the Symbols palette on all the symbols you'd like to work on.

NEW SYMBOL AND INSTANCE

Normally when you drag-and-drop a selected object into the Symbols palette (Window> Symbols), a new symbol is created, but the original artwork has no connection to the symbol—the artwork is not an instance, meaning all its paths are still editable. To create a new symbol *and* turn the original object into an instance of the new symbol, press-and-hold the Shift key as you drag the artwork into the Symbols palette.

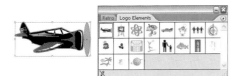   

Artwork not a symbol instance   *Artwork as a symbol instance*

SELECT ALL INSTANCES (AND REPLACE THEM TOO)

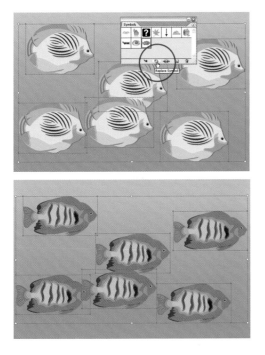

You can create multiple instances of a symbol by placing copies (Edit>Copy; Edit>Paste), or using the Selection tool (V) to select an instance and pressing-and-holding the Option key (PC: Alt key) while dragging to make a copy. But to select all the instances of a symbol in the document, make sure you have nothing selected in your document and click on the symbol in the Symbols palette. Then use the palette's flyout menu to choose Select All Instances. If you want to replace all the selected instances, click on the new symbol in the Symbols palette and press the Replace Symbol icon (the second icon from the left) at the bottom of the palette.

REPLACING SYMBOLS

You know by now (if you read the previous tip) that you can replace all instances of a symbol. What we haven't told you yet is that if you applied effects, changed colors with the Symbol Stainer tool, or resized the instance, all those characteristics will be preserved when you replace the symbol with a new one. For example, in our original symbol instance using the planets, we applied various effects and used the Symbol Stainer tool. When we replaced the symbol (see previous tip), all the instances changed to the cat symbol, while still preserving their individual characteristics.

REVERSE ENGINEERING A GRAPHIC STYLE

One of the best ways to learn all the great things you can do with graphic styles is to apply an existing style and then check out the Appearance palette (Window>Appearance). The entire makeup of the style will be laid out nicely for you—extra fills and strokes, effects, colors, and so on. In addition, if you really like a style and want to make a new one based on an existing style, you can of course, alter the style by selecting it in the Graphic Styles palette and changing style items in the Appearance palette. Then just click the New Graphic Style icon at the bottom of the Graphic Styles palette.

WHY ARE SOME FILTERS AND EFFECTS GRAYED OUT?

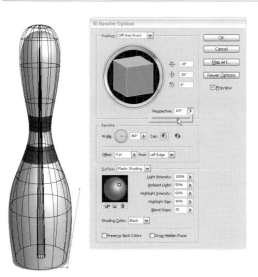

If you attempt to access a filter or an effect and it's unavailable (grayed out), there could be several reasons. The bottom half of the Filter menu (from Artistic down) only works on rasterized objects or placed raster images. Moreover, many of the filters only work in RGB mode. Similarly, many Effect menu commands will only work if the document is in RGB mode. As you may know from a previous tip, you cannot switch from CMYK mode to RGB, apply an Effect menu command, and then switch back to CMYK because the effect will be lost.

SEE 3D EFFECTS WHILE YOU'RE APPLYING THEM

You may not have even noticed this one but when you change settings in the 3D effects dialogs, the settings aren't rendered to the screen until you take your finger off the mouse button. This makes it difficult to see what various settings look like as you're applying them. To get around this, hold down the Shift key as you modify a 3D graphic, and the view on screen will be re-rendered each time you move the setting.

ROTATE 3D OBJECTS THE RIGHT WAY

If you've tried to use the Rotate tool (R) on a 3D object, you may have noticed that the results can be somewhat unpredictable. Here's a tip: Do all of your rotating within the 3D effect dialog. This rotates the object in true 3D space and it'll leave things looking the way you expected.

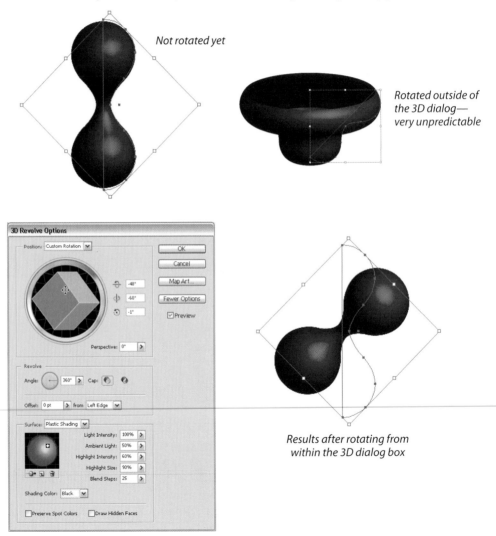

Not rotated yet

Rotated outside of the 3D dialog—very unpredictable

Results after rotating from within the 3D dialog box

Use the 3D Options dialog to rotate instead

CREATING A 3D BANNER

Here's a quick way to create a realistic banner using 3D effects. First, envision what the banner would look like if you were looking straight down at it. Easier said than done, we know. The good news is that you can just draw a path as you see here. Set the Fill for this path to None and change the stroke color to whatever color you'd like the banner to be. Next, choose Effects>3D>Extrude & Bevel. Adjust the Extrude setting in the resulting 3D Options dialog to give some depth to the banner, and move the rotate cube so the banner is facing you. Be sure to check the Preview button so that you can see the changes. That's it. Now you've got a shaded banner without going through all of the hassle of drawing each part manually.

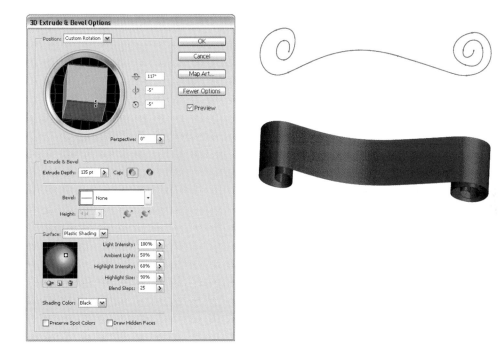

ADDING TEXT TO THE BANNER

What's a banner in the previous tip without text right? To add text to the banner, simply create the type that you'd like to have flow along the banner. Then drag the text into the Symbols palette (Window>Symbols) to make it a symbol. Now, select the banner and look in the Appearance palette (Window>Appearance). Double-click the 3D Extrude & Bevel item to modify the 3D effect you used to create the banner. Click the Map Art button and cycle through the Surfaces until you find the one of the front of the banner (look at the red highlights on the actual banner to see what surface is currently selected). Then, choose the new text symbol you just created from the Symbols pop-up menu. Position the text as you see fit, and keep in mind that it has a bounding box around it so you can transform it any way you'd like.

GET YOUR ARTWORK IN 3D

One of the interesting features of the Effect menu's 3D command is the option to map art onto 3D surfaces. Only symbols can be mapped to the surface, so before heading to the Effect menu, create a symbol that you want to map to the surface of your 3D object, and drag it into the Symbols palette. You can create some very interesting results by using a placed photo as your symbol. Yes, placed raster images can be turned into symbols as long as the images are embedded rather than linked. Try placing (File>Place) an image of a world map (to embed the image, make sure the Link checkbox isn't selected in the Place dialog). Make the image a symbol by dragging-and-dropping it into the Symbols palette (Window>Symbols). Then create a half-circle (by drawing a circle with the Ellipse tool [L] and cutting it in half with the Scissors tool [C]). Next, select your path and choose Effect>3D>Revolve. Click the Map Art button, select your symbol from the Symbol drop-down menu, and size the map to fit the grid by clicking the Scale to Fit button. You can add your symbol to different sides of the shape by using the Surface field. So now, if you ever need to show a different part of the world, double-click on the 3D Revolve effect in the Appearance palette, and use the 3D Revolve Options dialog to change the orientation of your globe.

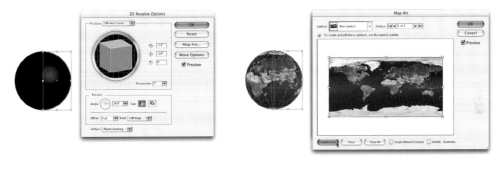

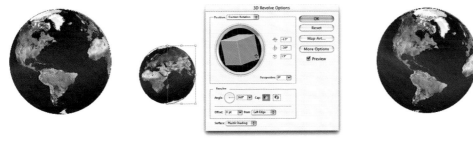

 **3D AS A STYLE**

You can make any of the 3D effects part of a graphic style, but you'll need to do one extra step if you want the color to be part of the style. Apply the 3D effect to your object by selecting it and choosing a command from the Effect>3D menu. Then go to the Appearance palette's flyout menu and choose Add New Fill. Even if your object already has a fill indicated, you'll need to add this second fill for it to register as part of the style. Then go the Graphic Style palette and use the flyout menu to choose New Graphic Style. Give your style a name, click OK, and you're set.

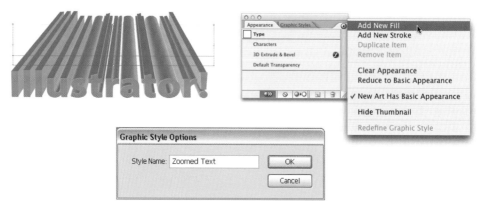

STAIN REMOVAL

After you've used the Symbol Stainer tool (which is nested under the Symbol Sprayer tool in the Toolbox) to change the color of a symbol, while you still have your symbol instances selected, hold down the Option key (PC: Alt key) to decrease the colorization amount and reveal more of the symbol's original color.

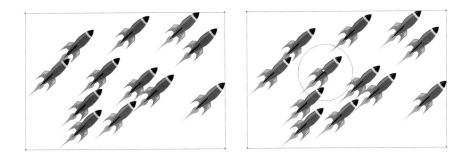

SCATTER BRUSH OPTIONS

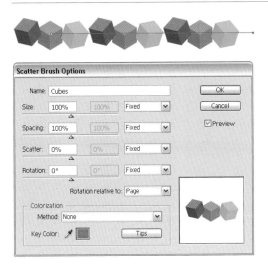

There are quite a few factors that determine exactly how a Scatter brush scatters along a path. Rather than trying to figure out the settings you need to create a brush, try this: Select the artwork for your brush and drag-and-drop it into the Brushes palette. When prompted, choose New Scatter Brush. Click OK in the Scatter Brush Options dialog without making any changes. Draw a short, open path with the Line tool and click on the new brush to apply it to the path. With the path still selected, double-click on the new brush in the Brushes palette to open the Scatter Brush Options dialog. Check the Preview box and now you can choose your settings, taking advantage of the preview to see what settings work best.

 **SCATTER ENHANCERS**

When a Scatter brush's options are set at Random (rather than Fixed), you specify a range of numbers to determine the randomness of the Size, Spacing, Scatter, and Rotation settings. If you're editing these Random settings in the Scatter Brush Options dialog, you can make your life a little easier with these keys. Double-click your Scatter brush to get the dialog, then press-and-hold the Option key (PC: Alt key) to move the minimum and maximum percentage an equal distance apart for one of the settings. For example, if the Spacing slider is set to 100% Fixed and you choose Random in the pop-up menu, hold down Option/Alt and drag the triangle slider to change the minimum to 150% and the maximum to 50% (with nothing held down you'd have to move each slider independently). Once you've set the range you'd like to use, you can move the range higher or lower (while keeping the same distance between the sliders) by holding down the Shift key. (Careful, this last step can be a bit touchy. Try it out and you'll see what we mean.)

 **SYMBOL STACKING ORDER**

You can change the stacking order of multiple symbols using the Symbol Shifter tool—that is, as long as you have already selected the instances in the Symbols palette (Window>Symbols). To bring symbol instances forward, Shift-click the symbol instance with the Symbol Shifter tool (nested under the Symbol Sprayer in the Toolbox). To send the symbol instances backward, press-and-hold Option-Shift (PC: Alt-Shift) and click the symbol instance.

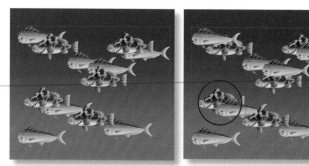

Symbols brought forward   *Symbols sent to back*

MAKE YOUR OWN BEVELS FOR 3D

If you really want to experiment with the Extrude & Bevel 3D effect, try this: Open the document called Bevels.ai that is located in the Illustrator CS2 application's Plug-ins folder. Draw a short, angled line with the Pen (P) or Line (\) tool and drag the path into the Symbols palette (Window>Symbols) to create a symbol. Save the document, close it, and restart Illustrator. Then, when you choose Effect>3D>Extrude & Bevel, your new bevel will appear in the dialog's Bevel pop-up menu. With a bit of experimentation (each time adding a symbol to Bevels.ai, saving the document, and restarting Illustrator), you can create some pretty interesting results.

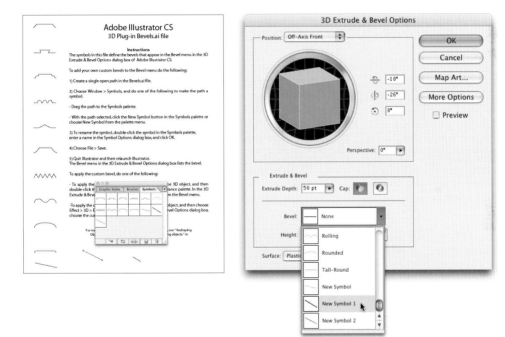

STAIN REPELLANT

This is a pretty basic concept, but if you try to use the Symbol Stainer tool (nested under the Symbol Sprayer in the Toolbox) and nothing happens, it's because the Symbol Stainer tool cannot affect an object that is black. With this in mind, you might want to create a version of your symbol in shades of gray and drag-and-drop it into the Symbols palette. Then if you decide to stain the symbol, you'll have a version on which the Symbol Stainer tool will work.

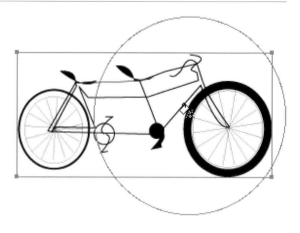

GETTING MORE SYMBOLS IN ILLUSTRATOR

Although Illustrator CS2 comes with a decent selection of symbol libraries, you can easily add many more symbols by using the brush libraries (because there are many more brush libraries included). From the Brushes palette's flyout menu, choose Open Brush Libraries and pick a library (we selected Decorative Scatter). From the library palette that appears, drag a brush onto the artboard and then drag-and-drop it into the Symbols palette. Voilà! New symbol.

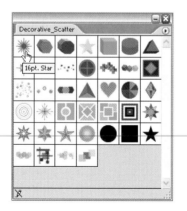
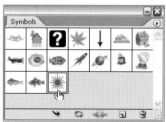

FREE! 1,000+ SCIENTIFIC SYMBOLS FOR ILLUSTRATOR

This will possibly be the most read tip in this book. Why? Because it has the word "FREE" in it. Anyway… here's a useful download tip with a ton of free symbols for Illustrator. The Integration and Application Network at the University of Maryland Center for Environmental Science has produced a series of scientific symbol libraries. The libraries contain more than 1,000 custom-made symbols (in 28 categories) designed specifically for enhancing science communication skills for the graphically challenged. Diagrammatic representations of complex processes can be developed easily with minimal graphical skills. The best part about it is the libraries are available cost and royalty free. You can also download a searchable index (PDF) of all the available symbols and an interactive flash tutorial on how to use the symbols with Adobe Illustrator (they require version 10.0 or better). Just go to: http://ian.umces.edu/index.html?http&&&ian.umces.edu/conceptualdiagrams.php and check it out.

BRUSH OPTIONS VS. OPTIONS OF SELECTED OBJECT

When you want to apply an Art brush to the stroke of an object, there are a couple of different options dialogs that can help you. Double-click on an Art brush in the Brushes palette (Window>Brushes) to set the overall options for the brush—every time you use the brush it will use these settings. Or, to affect only the selected object, select the object, click on the Art brush in the palette to apply the stroke, and click the Options of Selected Object icon at the bottom of the Brushes palette. Change the setting to affect how the brush stroke is applied to only that object. (The same principle applies to Scatter brushes and Calligraphic brushes.)

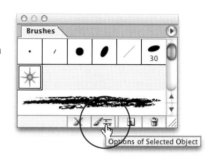

BIRTHDAY BRUSH

There's an Easter Egg hidden in the Calligraphic Brush Options dialog that was revealed by Deke McClelland in his *Real World Adobe Illustrator* book. Why is it called an Easter Egg? Because it's a little hidden treat that serves no practical purpose whatsoever. Double-click on any Calligraphic brush to open the options dialog and enter these settings: Angle 5°, Roundness 26%, and Diameter 56 points. Click anywhere in the dialog, and you'll get a birthday surprise. Does the brush actually paint with this special design? No, thus the Easter Egg designation—cool but no practical application.

If a picture's worth a thousand words, how *much of a picture can 37 words create? If sticks and stones can break my bones, but words*

Trading Spaces
text, text, text

can never hurt me, what in fact is the value of words? It's easy to underestimate the power of text, especially when we're discussing a graphics program like Illustrator. Strange as it may seem, Illustrator's powerful text capabilities can actually create an image—in words—that's worth as much as any picture. So with all that in mind, we decided to present this entire chapter only in pictures, without words. Okay, so that lasted for the first two tips and then we quickly returned to the more traditional words, accompanied by a picture method. It was an interesting thought though, wasn't it?

 **SELECTING TEXT**

For the most part, selecting text in Illustrator CS2 is similar to most applications: Double-click on a word with the Type tool (T) to select it; triple-click to select the entire paragraph (as we did in our example).

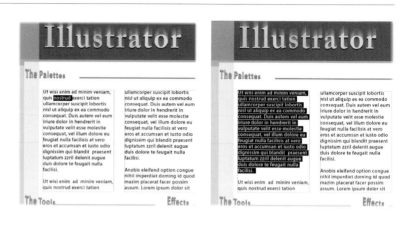

To select a portion of a paragraph (without clicking-and-dragging), there are a couple of options. Hold down the Shift key and press the Right Arrow key, or click once at the beginning of the text, hold down Shift and click at the end of the text you want to select.

 **PICKING THE NEXT WORD**

To move the insertion point to the start of the previous word, press Command (PC: Control) and the Left Arrow key. We know you'd never guess this, but believe it or not, press Command (PC: Control) and the Right Arrow key to move the text insertion point to the start of the next word (as we did in our example here).

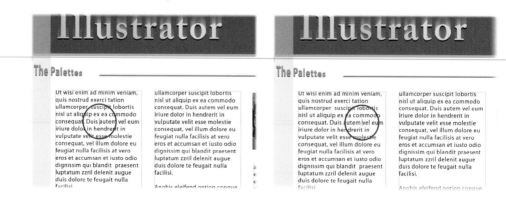

SELECT BY PARAGRAPHS

One of the great things about these techniques is that you'll get slightly different results depending on the image you use. Try it with a variety of images.

Background #1:
Use the Motion Blur filter with the distance set to the maximum distance: 999 pixels. Of course you can experiment with the distance settings if you wish.

Background #2:
On the top layer, apply the Motion Blur filter as in the first example. To the bottom layer, you'll also apply the Motion Blur filter, but this time with a lower amount for the distance setting (200–400 pixels) and a different angle.

One of the great things about these techniques is that you'll get slightly different results depending on the image you use. Try it with a variety of images.

Background #1:
Use the Motion Blur filter with the distance set to the maximum distance: 999 pixels. Of course you can experiment with the distance settings if you wish.

Background #2:
On the top layer, apply the Motion Blur filter as in the first example. To the bottom layer, you'll also apply the Motion Blur filter, but this time with a lower amount for the distance setting (200–400 pixels) and a different angle.

To select a paragraph, try this. Press Shift-Command-Down Arrow key (PC: Shift-Control-Down Arrow key) to select from the current text insertion to the end of the current paragraph. Press Shift-Command-Up Arrow key (PC: Shift-Control-Up Arrow key) to select from the current text insertion to the beginning of the current paragraph. To select the paragraph above or below your current selection, use the shortcut and continue to press the Up or Down Arrow keys, with the Down Arrow key selecting the next paragraph and the Up Arrow key selecting the previous paragraph.

CHANGE THE DEFAULT FONT IN ILLUSTRATOR

In case you haven't realized yet, the default font in Illustrator is Myriad. This font is selected in the Font menu, Character palette, and as the Normal Character Style in the Character Styles palette. It is selected even if the document you open doesn't contain that font or if you last used another font before quitting Illustrator. Are you seeing a pattern here? For some reason, Adobe wants us to use Myriad. Heck, it's a nice font, so they may be right. But if this bugs you, then you can always change the default font by editing the startup files. It's a little tricky, but hey… if it really bugs you, then it may be worth it. To change the default font:

1. Quit Illustrator.
2. In the Adobe Illustrator CS2\Plug-ins folder, duplicate the current default startup file—Adobe Illustrator Startup_CMYK or Adobe Illustrator Startup_RGB—and give it a different name. (This creates a copy of the original startup file in case you need it again.)
3. Open one of the default startup files (Adobe Illustrator Startup_CMYK or Adobe Illustrator Startup_RGB, depending on which type of document you intend to use).
4. Choose Window>Type>Character Styles.
5. Select the Normal Character Style and choose Character Style Options from the palette's flyout menu.
6. Select Basic Character Formats on the left side of the dialog, and choose the desired font from the Font Family menu.
7. Click OK, and save the new file as Adobe Illustrator Startup_CMYK or Adobe Illustrator Startup_RGB in the Plug-ins folder.
8. Restart Illustrator.

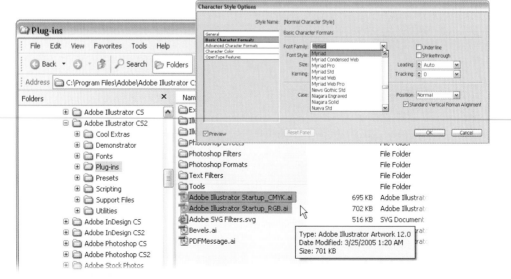

PICK A FONT BY NAME

If you have a big long list of fonts, it can take a while to scroll through the list to find the one you want. Instead, get the Character palette from the Window menu and click just to the left of the font name that appears in the palette. Type the first letter or two of the font name you want (as we did here with Trajan Pro). You'll jump to the first font that matches the letters you type.

MOVE ALL TABS AT ONCE

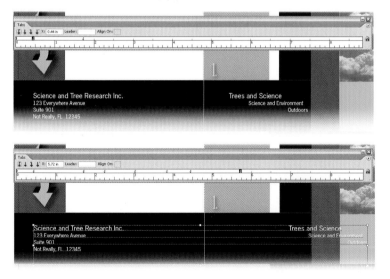

When you're creating a table using the Tabs palette, you may need to move a tab stop, but you still want to keep the rest of your tabs evenly spaced. To do this, first make sure you have the palette open by choosing Type>Tabs from the Window menu (Command-Shift-T [PC: Control-Shift-T]), then select your table with the Selection tool (V), and while pressing the Command key (PC: Control key), drag the tab stop you need to move. In the Tabs palette, all the tab stops to the right of the one you're dragging will also move, preserving the space between them.

 **CHANGE TAB STYLE**

Illustrator lets you add tab stops for left-, center-, right-, and decimal-justi-fied text. Once you have added a tab stop above the Tab Ruler in the Tabs palette (Window>Type>Tabs), you can quickly change between the different tab styles by Option-clicking (PC: Alt-clicking) on the existing tab stop. Each time you click, the tab stop will change to the next style (left-justified, center-justified, etc.).

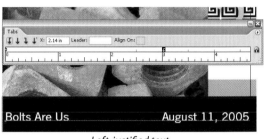

Left-justified text

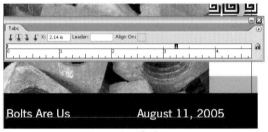

Center-justified text

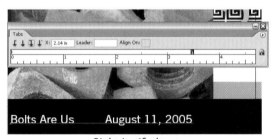

Right-justified text

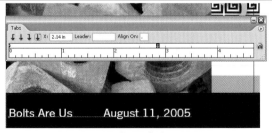

Decimal-justified text

DELETE ALL TABS

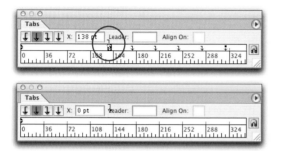

To delete a tab stop in the Tabs palette (Command-Shift-T [PC: Control-Shift-T]), you click-and-drag it off the Tab Ruler. Rather than manually dragging every tab stop to delete them all, hold down the Command key (PC: Control key) and click-and-drag the left-most tab stop off the Tab Ruler. All tab stops will be deleted. Use the same theory anytime you need to delete all the tab stops to the right of a tab stop: Press-and-hold the Command key (PC: Control key) and click-and-drag the first tab stop you want to delete off the palette and all the tab stops to the right of that tab stop will be deleted.

EVENLY SPACED TABS

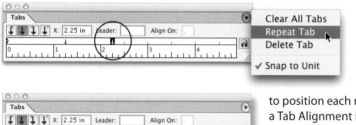

If you need a bunch of tab stops evenly spaced apart, there's an easier way than "doing the math" and figuring out where to position each new tab stop. Select a Tab Alignment icon from the row of four icons near the top left of the Tabs palette, click above the ruler to add the first and then the second tab stop, using the space you want between the two. Then, with your last tab stop still selected, choose Repeat Tab from the Tabs palette's flyout menu to create a whole series of evenly spaced tab stops. (The new, nicely spaced tab stops will appear as wide as you make the Tab Ruler in the Tabs palette. To extend the Tabs Ruler, just click on the bottom-right corner of the palette and drag to the right.)

TAB LEADERS

A nice feature in Illustrator CS2 is tab leaders, which provide the ability to fill the space between the type and the tab with a text character. Click on a tab stop in the Tabs palette, enter a character in the Leader field (such as a period), and then press Return (PC: Enter) or Tab to see the results. You can actually enter up to eight characters in the Leader field, so the possibilities are pretty interesting.

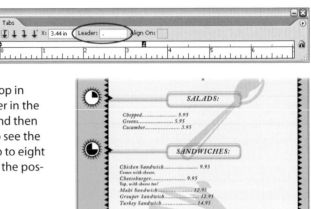

LINE UP THE TAB RULER

When you have a series of text blocks throughout your document and many or all of them use tabs, you'll need to move the Tabs palette (Command-Shift-T [PC: Control-Shift-T]) from one text block to the next to see the Tab Ruler, and edit the tab stops. Rather than dragging the Tabs palette above each text block, just select the text block with either the Type tool (T) or Selection tool (V), and in the Tabs palette, click on the magnet icon along the palette's right side (aka: the Position Palette Above Text icon, but who wants to say that?). The Tabs palette will automatically line up perfectly above the selected text block.

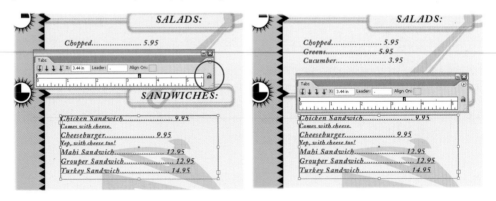

ALIGN ON

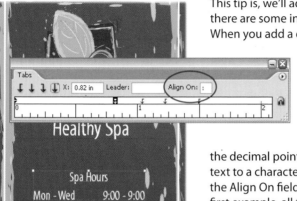

This tip is, we'll admit, a little out there, but there are some interesting uses for this concept. When you add a decimal-aligned tab stop to the Tab Ruler in the Tabs palette (Window>Type>Tabs), by default Illustrator assumes that you want the text to align using the decimal point (a fair assumption). You don't have to be satisfied with aligning to the decimal point, but instead you can align your text to a character by entering any character in the Align On field at the top of the palette. In our first example, all the tabbed text is aligning to the semi-colons, so the workout times all line up. The second example is a little more unusual, with all the words aligning on the letter "a" in each word.

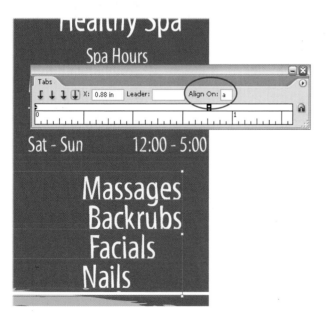

ANGLED TABS

With a bit of effort, you can create what amounts to graphical tabs. Create a text frame with the Type tool (T) and fill it with text information, separating the text with tab stops by using the Tabs palette (or by simply pressing the Tab key as you type information). Then get the Pen (P) or Line (\) tool from the Toolbox and draw paths that will replace the tab stops. You can give your paths a stroke color, such as black, but you should avoid a fill color so you can see the effect you're about to create. Select the paths and the text frame with the Selection tool (V), and from the Object menu choose Text Wrap>Make. Click OK if you get a warning dialog; this is just letting you know that text will be altered. The tabbed text will line up with the paths. To change the text offset or invert the wrap, go to Object>Text Wrap and choose Text Wrap Options. You also may need to use the Direct Selection tool (A) and perform some tweaking to get the ideal result, as we did in our example here.

	sprockets	widgets	ipods
jan	12	15	18
feb	91	11	13
mar	33	22	11
apr	56	60	87
may	11	12	13
jun	12	15	18
jul	71	31	43
aug	40	28	19
sep	55	56	63
nov	10	10	18

SCROLL THE VIEW WITH TEXT

With most tools, pressing the Spacebar temporarily gives you the Hand tool so you can navigate in the document. Try that while you're typing and, of course, you get spaces. So how do you do that temporary Hand tool thing when you're typing? Press Command-Spacebar (PC: Alt-Spacebar), the shortcut for the Zoom tool. Once the cursor has changed to the Zoom tool, let go of the Command key (PC: Control key), and you'll have the Hand tool, ready to navigate. Let go and you're right back to typing again.

QUICK EDIT

Here's a quick way to switch between the Selection tool and the Type tool, allowing you to start editing some text. Using the Selection tool (V) or the Direct Selection tool (A), double-click on some type. The Type tool will be activated and the text insertion point will appear in the location where you clicked.

 HANGING INDENTS

To create hanging indents easily, select your text with the Type tool (T), go to the Window menu, select Paragraph, and use this formula in the Paragraph palette: Enter a positive value

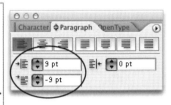

Illustrator has a long memory when it comes to text settings, so if you have changed indents, baseline shift, etc., you have in effect changed the default settings.

in the Left Indent field, and in the First-Line Left Indent field (right below the Left Indent field), enter the same value with a minus sign in front to make it a negative value. Once you get it to work just right, create a paragraph style by choosing Type>Paragraph Style from the Window menu. In the palette that appears, choose New Paragraph Style from the flyout menu. Now you can select your style in the Paragraph Styles palette, and you don't have to go through all that formatting again.

 RESET ALL SETTINGS

Illustrator has a long memory when it comes to text settings, so if you have changed indents, baseline shift, etc., you have in effect, changed the default settings. To make sure you don't get unexpected results, you probably want to deselect the text and then either manually change the settings back to "normal," or use the type palette's flyout menu and choose Reset Palette. You'll need to do this for both the Character and Paragraph palettes.

COLORED TEXT, COLORED BOX

Selected text filled with white   *Text object filled with black*

When you create area type, there are two different objects that can be colored: the type itself and the box that contains the type. To change the fill color of the type, go to the Toolbox, click on the Fill color swatch, and get the Selection tool (V). Then click on the text object and choose a fill color from either the Color or Swatches palette. Use the Direct Selection tool (A) to change a text object's color without affecting the text. First, click away from the object to deselect it, then click directly on the path of the object (typically the text frame). Now when you choose a fill color from the Color or Swatches palette, you will fill the text object, not the text.

HORIZONTAL TO VERTICAL TYPE

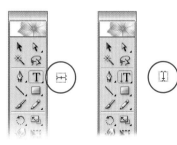

Before using the Type tool (T), you can change from the regular horizontal Type tool to the Vertical Type tool by holding down the Shift key before clicking on the art-board (notice your cursor changes direction). As you may have guessed, the Shift key also works the opposite way if you've selected the Vertical Type tool from the Toolbox. The Vertical Type tool will change into the regular Type tool when you Shift-click.

KERN FROM THE KEYBOARD

Adjusting the space between a pair of letters is known as kerning (yes, you probably knew that, but we needed to be sure). To adjust the kerning between two letters, click between the two letters with the Type tool (T), press-and-hold the Option key (PC: Alt key), and use the Right Arrow key

Increasing the kerning between the R and E

to increase the kerning or the Left Arrow key to decrease the kerning. To change the kerning using larger increments, add in the Command key (PC: Control key), making the shortcut Command-Option-Right (or Left) Arrow key (PC: Control-Alt-Right [or Left] Arrow key), depending on whether you're increasing or decreasing the kerning.

TRACKING WITH THE KEYBOARD

Tracking loosens or tightens the amount of space between selected text or a full block of text (again, sorry if that's old news to you). The shortcuts to adjust the tracking with the keyboard are the

Tracking decreased

Tracking increased

same as with kerning, except to select a range of text. Highlight all the text you want to adjust using the Type tool (T), press-and-hold the Option key (PC: Alt key), and use the Right Arrow key to increase tracking or the Left Arrow key to decrease tracking. To change the tracking using larger increments, press Command-Option-Right (or Left) Arrow key (PC: Control-Alt-Right [or Left] Arrow key) while you have your text block selected.

CONTROL NUMBER OF RECENT FONTS

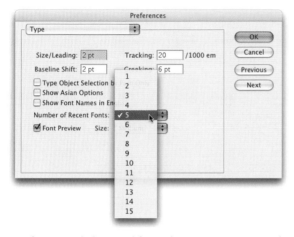

One of the newer options in Illustrator CS2 is to view the most recent fonts you've used in Illustrator. That is, you're not just seeing the fonts you used in the current document, but the fonts you've used since you last launched Illustrator. If you open a new document, your most recent fonts show up in the list under Type>Recent Fonts. You can control how many fonts display in the list through Illustrator's Preferences. Press Command-K (PC: Control-K) to open the Preferences dialog, and from the pop-up menu in the top-left corner, choose Type. Pick a number from 1–15 in the Number of Recent Fonts pop-up menu.

FONT PREVIEW—OR NOT

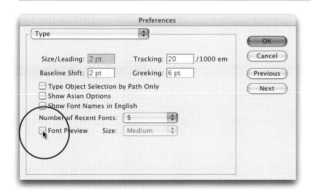

The ability to see the typefaces in the font list is a personal choice: Some people like the option to see what all their fonts look like in the Character palette (Window>Type>Character), others don't like the slight slow down in the font list. To turn off this preview in the font list, go to Illustrator's Preferences (Command-K [PC: Control-K]) and choose Type from the pop-up menu in the top-left corner of the dialog. The checkbox to the left of the Font Preview Size pop-up menu turns the preview on and off.

RESET KERNING AND TRACKING

We showed you in an earlier tip how to reset all the settings in the Character and Paragraph palettes (choosing Reset Palette from the respective palette's flyout menu). If you want to keep everything else as-is but reset just the kerning and tracking to zero, here's how: To reset the tracking, highlight your text with the Type tool (T) and press Command-Option-Q (PC: Control-Alt-Q). To reset the kerning, click the Type tool where you've adjusted the kerning and use the same shortcut. Needless to say, make sure you've got the Option (PC: Alt) key held down, or you'll get a very different result!

OPEN AND START EDITING

Here's a cool way to jump right into formatting your text if the Character palette isn't visible—or even open. Press Command-Option-Shift-M (PC: Control-Alt-Shift-M) to highlight the font field in the Character palette, which will also open the palette if necessary (whether you're using the Type tool or not).

EDIT IMPORTED TEXT

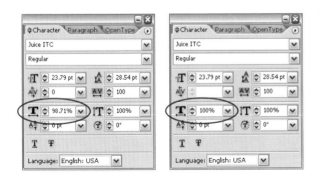

Chances are the text that someone typed for you may not be ideal—perhaps they used two spaces after a period, or typed in inches symbols rather than quotation marks. After placing the text file (File>Place), get Illustrator to automatically strip out all errors using Smart Punctuation. Select the text with either the Selection (V) or Type (T) tool, choose Smart Punctuation from the Type menu, then check the items you want to replace in the resulting dialog.

RESET HORIZONTAL SCALING

To reset just the Horizontal Scale field to its default setting of 100%, without affecting all the other text settings in the Character palette (Window>Type>Character), press Command-Shift-X (PC: Control-Shift-X). You can use this tip to reset the horizontal scaling of an entire selected text block or to simply change the setting in the Character palette before you create another text object.

SET LEADING TO THE FONT SIZE

Here's a quick way to set the leading (the space between lines of type) to the same size as the current font size: Highlight your text with the Type tool (T), double-click on the Leading icon in the Character palette (just to the left of the Leading field). Just in case you're interested, equal font and leading sizes is known as solid leading, and it works best when your text is in all caps, so there are no descenders to bump into the type below.

INCREASE OR DECREASE LEADING

To quickly increase or decrease the leading, select text with either the Selection (V) or Type (T) tool and press Option-Up or Down Arrow (PC: Alt-Up or Down Arrow). At first it might seem a little counter-intuitive because the Down Arrow key increases leading (in most palette fields, the Down Arrow makes values smaller). But when you think about it, it makes perfect sense—increased leading makes the second line of type move down, therefore we use the Down Arrow key to increase leading. Here's where it gets a little weird: If you click in the Leading field in the Character palette, the Up and Down Arrow keys work like all the other fields, so you would press the Up Arrow key to increase leading! It's all very logical—really it is!

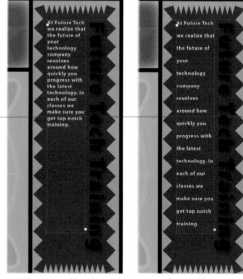

Decreased leading   Increased leading

CONVERT PARAGRAPH TEXT

Unfortunately, there is no command to convert paragraph text (that is, text you've created using a text box) into regular point type (meaning type that is not confined to a text box). You'll have to do this conversion yourself by highlighting all the text in the text frame with the Type tool (T) and cutting it using the Command-X (PC: Control-X) keyboard shortcut. Then, deselecting the text box (Command-Shift-A [PC: Control-Shift-A]) and clicking with the Type tool on the artboard. This creates a new, single text insertion point and you can press Command-V (PC: Control-V) to paste the text. (You can tell the difference by clicking on the text with the Direct Selection tool (A), which will show a text bounding-box or a path, as seen here.)

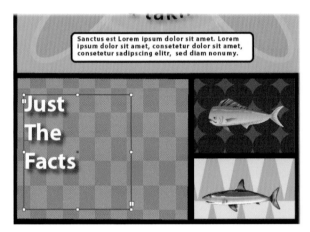

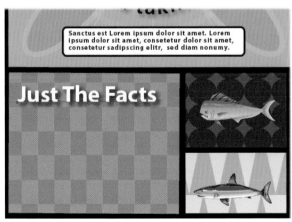

 CLEANING UP YOUR TEXT

Each time you click with the Type tool (T) and then decide not to add type after all, you may be adding small text insertion points that could end up causing you grief. You won't see these points in Preview mode, but if you switch to Outline mode from the View menu, you'll see a little X for each insertion point. To automatically remove all of the extra points, go to the Object menu and choose Path>Clean Up. In the dialog, make sure that Empty Text Paths is checked and then click OK. All those unnecessary—potentially troublesome—empty text points will go away.

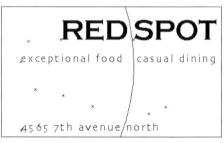

Image in Preview mode   *Image in Outline mode*

MAKE YOUR OWN TYPEFACE

Okay, it's not exactly making a typeface, but it's a pretty cool way to change the look of type in a way that's very flexible. Enter some text with the Type tool (T), select it with the Selection tool (V), and from the Effect menu choose Stylize>Round Corners. Check the Preview check-box and then experiment with the Radius field using the Up and Down Arrow keys to get the result you want. Of course, the effect can always be edited by double-clicking the words Rounded Corners in the Appearance palette.

If the sharks don't get ya first our food will!

If the sharks don't get ya first our food will!

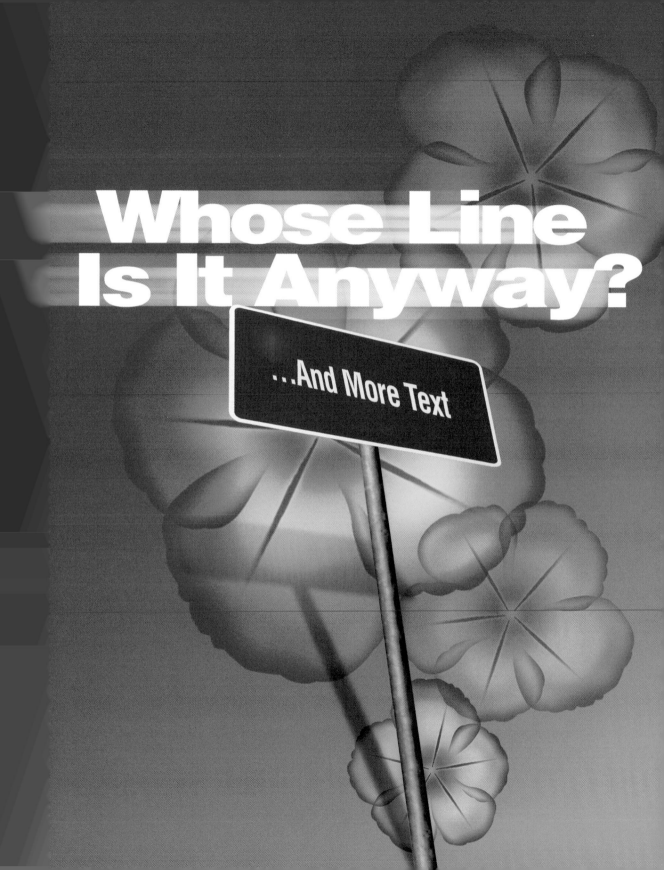

When we were planning the structure of this book, everyone was telling us that it really should have at least ten chapters. Why?

Whose Line Is It Anyway?
...and more text

Apparently, ten is some mystical number that instills confidence in book-buyers, giving them a heightened sense of comfort in their purchase. Problem was, we had pretty much determined the chapters we wanted, giving the book the logical divisions that we felt it needed. "Sorry," we told them, "Nine chapters is all you're going to get, but they will be nine memorable chapters, you can be sure of that!" Well, our stance of "nine is enough" was met with looks of amusement as we were introduced to a new member of the book-editing team. Saying his name aloud brings back too many painful memories, so let us instead introduce Chapter 10, the other half of what we originally had planned as Chapter 9 (and we have to admit it, it was a good call).

TRANSFORMING TYPE

Ever notice that you can't use all of the features of the Free Transform tool (E) when you're working with type? You won't be able to use the Command key (PC: Control key) to skew or warp it in certain ways. If you want to do this with the

Free Transform tool, you'll first have to convert the type to outlines by selecting it and choosing Type>Create Outlines. Now you're free to transform away.

DRAG-AND-DROP TEXT FROM DESKTOP

One simple way to add text to an Illustrator document is to drag-and-drop a text document from the desktop into the artwork—just make sure you hold down the Shift key as you drag in the text file. A text block will be created that contains all the text.

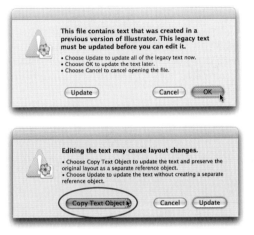

BEFORE AND AFTER LEGACY TEXT

When you open documents from previous versions of Illustrator that contain type, you'll get a warning about updating the legacy text. Although you could choose to update all the text at once, you will not be able to see the difference between the legacy text and the updated text in CS2. Instead, click OK and then update individual pieces of text by using the Type tool (T) to click on the text you want to edit. In the dialog that appears, click the Copy Text Object button and a dimmed copy of the original (legacy) text will appear below the updated text. Use the original text for comparison as you manually adjust the updated type to match the original. Once you're done, go to the Type menu, choose Legacy Text, and from the submenu, choose to hide or delete the copy that was created for you.

I asked another boy about his daddy. He frowned and started to cry. And when I asked him what was wrong, this was the boy's reply. "My Daddy is only a picture in a frame that hangs on the wall. each day I talk to my Daddy, but he never talks at all. I tell him all of my secrets, and all of my little plans. And from the way he smiles at me, I know he understands."

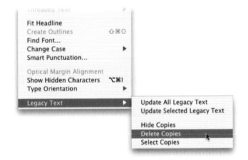

TYPE SIZE BY MATH

For those times where you just don't want to "do the math" yourself, let Illustrator do it for you. In the Font Size field of the Character palette (Window>Character), type * (for multiply) and the number (we used 1.5 in our example). Press Return (PC: Enter) and Illustrator will do the math for you. In our case, change 9-point type to 13.5 points. Use * for Multiply and / for Divide—just remember to click after the unit of measurement.

GRADIENT-FILLED TEXT

In order to fill text with a gradient, you cannot simply click on a gradient swatch. Too bad…but there is an easy solution that you can use over and over again. Create an object and fill it with your chosen gradient by clicking on a gradient swatch in the Swatches palette (Window>Swatches). Then with the Selection tool (V), drag the object into the Graphic Styles palette (Windows>Graphic Styles) or choose New Graphic Style from the palette's flyout menu. Now, anytime you need to fill some text with the gradient, just select your text with the Selection tool, and click the gradient in the Graphic Styles palette, applying it to your text. You can still edit the type with the Type tool (T) and change the direction of the gradient using the Gradient tool (G) from the Toolbox. This is simple but effective; especially since you can reuse the graphic style anytime you need it.

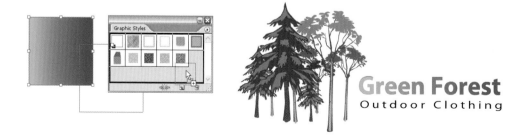

HIDE THE HIGHLIGHT

When you highlight a word using the Type tool (T) and attempt to change its color, the highlight ends up giving you an inversed color effect for the type. So, to keep the text highlighted and see the real color, press Command-H (PC: Control-H) to hide the highlight. Keep in mind that the text is still highlighted, but you just can't see the highlight (as in our example here, where our black type was inverted to white, but by using this tip, we hid the highlight so we could see the black type). Repeat the shortcut to show the highlight again.

CLEAR THE OVERRIDE

An override is any text attribute in the Character Styles palette (found under the Window menu under Type) that is not part of the style (such as changing the font size). When a style override is made, it is indicated in the Character Styles palette by a small plus sign (+) beside the character style name. To clear the override, select your text with the Selection (V) or Type (T) tool, hold down the Option key (PC: Alt key), and click on the style name in the palette. The selected text will be reformatted to the original character style attributes.

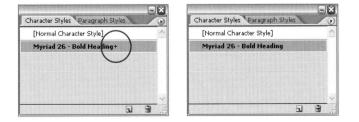

OVERRIDE THE OVERRIDE

When you apply a new style to some text (by selecting it and choosing a different character style from the Character Styles palette), any overrides will remain from the original style—even though you're changing the type's style. To clear overrides when applying a new style to selected type, press the Option key (PC: Alt key) as you click on the new style name in the Character Styles palette.

Original style *New style applied* *Overriding style*

LOAD STYLES FROM OTHER DOCUMENTS

Don't re-create character or paragraph styles when you can load them from another document. For example, go to the Character Styles palette's flyout menu (found under the Window menu under Type) and choose Load Character Styles. Then navigate to the document that contains the styles you need. You can choose to load just the character styles (or only the paragraph styles, if you're in the Paragraph Styles palette) or choose Load All Styles to load the document's character and paragraph styles while you're using either palette.

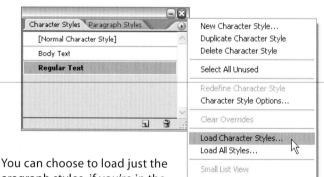

ANGLED MARGINS

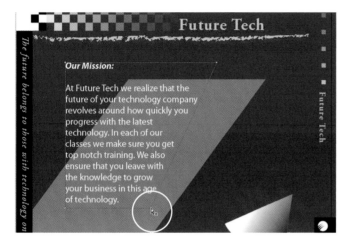

Need to create angled margins for a text box? It's pretty easy with the Direct Selection tool (A): Make sure *only* the text frame is selected with the Direct Selection tool and click on the corner anchor point where you would like to create the angle. Then drag the anchor point to the left or right to create an angle on that side of the text box.

CHARACTER ROTATION

The real tip here is to make sure you don't miss this feature because it's not in the standard view of the Character palette. It's called the Character Rotation field, and it lets you rotate characters (duh) relative to the baseline of the text. To access the control, make sure the Character palette is in its full view by choosing it from the Window menu under Type. When the palette appears, choose Show Options from the flyout menu. You can either highlight individual characters with the Type tool (T) or select an entire block of text with the Selection tool (V), and then pick an angle of rotation from the field's pop-up menu or enter the value you want in the field.

CONVERT WARPED TEXT TO OUTLINES

If you have warped some text—meaning you've selected it the with Selection tool (V), chosen Object>Envelope Distort>Make With Warp, and chosen a style, such as Arc—and now you want to convert the text to outlines (to send to someone who doesn't have that font, for example), you can't use the Type>Create Outlines command. Instead, when you have the warped text selected with the Selection tool, you'll have to use the Object>Expand command to create outlines of your type.

EDIT WARPED TEXT

If you have applied an envelope warp to a text object (Object>Envelope Distort>Make With Warp) and now you want to edit the text, press Command-Shift-V (PC: Control-Shift-V), or go to Object>Envelope Distort>Edit Contents. Once you've finished editing the text with the Type tool (T) and want to re-apply the warp, switch to the Selection tool, and press the same shortcut again.

TYPE ON A CIRCLE

In earlier versions of Illustrator, you could easily create type on both the top and bottom of a circle. You simply had to create the text on the top of the circle, hold down the Option key (PC: Alt key), and drag a copy to the bottom with the Selection tool (V). This shortcut doesn't work in Illustrator CS2. To work around this missing shortcut, do this: Draw a circle with the Ellipse tool (L) while holding the Shift key. Get the Type on a Path tool (which is nested under the Type tool in the Toolbox), click the Align Center icon in the Paragraph palette (found under the Window menu under Type), click on the bottom center of your circle, and enter your text. Your type will be centered at the top of the circle. With the Selection tool (V), select the circle. Then press Command-C (PC: Control-C) to copy and Command-F (PC: Control-F) for the Paste in Front command. Then, drag the copied text to the bottom of the circle by clicking-and-dragging the little line that is sticking up just above the center of your text (avoiding the bounding box). To flip the text so it's reading the correct way, just drag that same line across the path towards the center of the circle. Select the bottom text with the Type tool (T) to edit it, and with your text highlighted, use the Set the Baseline Shift field in the Character palette to position the text below the edge of the circle. (*Note:* Unlike earlier Illustrator versions, you'll have to manually switch to the Selection tool to drag and flip your text. If you switch to the Selection tool using the Command key [PC: Control key] shortcut, it will stop the text from flipping as you drag it.) It sounds like a lot of steps, but do it once…twice… eight times and you'll see how simple it can be.

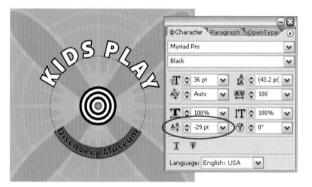

STOP FLIPPING

Okay, so this is the world's saddest excuse for a separate tip because it was just mentioned in the previous tip. But, just in case you didn't read the previous tip and jumped directly to this one, here we go: To stop text on a path from flipping over as you drag it with either the Selection tool (V) or Direct Selection tool (A), hold down the Command key (PC: Control key).

BASELINE SHIFT AMOUNT

Here's a pretty good guideline when you're applying a baseline shift to text on the bottom of a circle. With most fonts, simply enter a value in the Character palette's Set the Baseline Shift field that's approximately two-thirds of the font size. Highlight your text with the Type tool (T), highlight the Set the Baseline Shift field in the Character palette, enter minus (–) to move the text down, and enter the value that is two-thirds of the font size. (Remember to deselect the type and reset the Character palette's Set the Baseline Shift field back to zero when you're done, or else when you create new type, it will apply your last-used baseline shift setting.)

TYPE NOT ON A PATH

If you have created text on a path with the Type on a Path tool (nested under the Type tool in the Toolbox), and then later on decide you don't want it on the path, there is no command called "Remove text from the path." You'll have to do this by selecting just the text with the Type tool (T) and pressing Command-X (PC: Control-X) to cut it. Switch to the Selection tool, delete the path, and then click-and-drag with the Type tool to create a text box, and press Command-V (PC: Control-V) to paste.

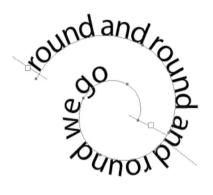

COPY FROM TEXT

You can use the Eyedropper tool (I) from the Toolbox to copy the attributes of existing text onto selected text. By default, the Eyedropper tool will copy fill, stroke, and other text attributes. (To see what your Eyedropper tool's options are, double-click the tool in the Toolbox.) Select the text you want to change with either the Selection (V) or Type (T) tool, and then use the Eyedropper tool to click on the text whose attributes you want to borrow. If you want to copy only the fill color, hold down the Shift key as you click with the Eyedropper tool on the text you're borrowing from.

THREAD TEXT INTO A NEW BOX

If you want to create threaded text (meaning you want to create linked text boxes that contain overflow text) and you want to ensure that the next text box is the same size as the first one, it's pretty simple. Select the text frame with the Selection tool (V), and click on the text frame's Out Port icon (located near the bottom-right corner) to load the overflow text—the cursor will change to the Loaded Text icon, which looks like a tiny newspaper page. Then click where you want the second text box to appear. The text is threaded into a new text box, and that box will be exactly the same size as the first text box in the thread. If you want the new text box to be a different size, click-and-drag to draw a box in the size you want while you have the Loaded Text icon showing as your cursor. When you release the mouse button, your text will flow into the box you created.

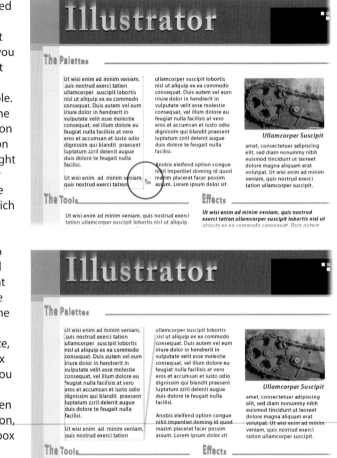

HIDE TEXT THREADS

Ullamcorper Suscipit

Text threads are Illustrator's way to show which text boxes are linked, allowing text to flow from one text box to the next. When you create text threads by using the Selection tool (V) and clicking on a text frame's Out Port icon (the tiny box near the bottom right of the text block), and then clicking on the In Port icon (the tiny box near the top left) of another text frame, Illustrator helps by showing a line that starts at the Out Port icon and ends at the In Port icon of the next text block. While this can be helpful to see where the text is flowing to, it can also be distracting; so to temporarily hide the thread lines for your selected text boxes, press Command-Shift-Y (PC: Control-Shift-Y). To show the thread lines, press the same keys again.

THREADED TEXT BLOCKS OF ANY SHAPE

Text can be threaded
between objects of
any shape, not just
rectangles. Draw a
shape using any of the
Shape tools (or even
the Pen tool [P]) from
the Toolbox, then click
directly on the path
of the shape with the

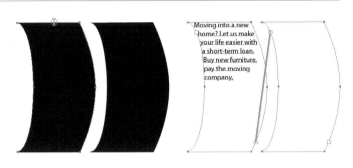

Area Type tool (which is nested under the Type tool in the Toolbox) to add some text inside
the shape. (*Note:* If your shape had any stroke or fill, those will disappear when you click with
the Area Type tool, which converts shapes automatically into text frames.) Create a second
shape, select both shapes with the Selection tool (V), and choose Threaded Text>Create
from the Type menu. It's magic!

STOP THE THREADING

If you created threaded text but then changed
your mind, you have a couple of options in the
Type>Threaded Text submenu. With your text
boxes selected, choose Remove Threading to
break the flow of the text—meaning no more
text will overflow into the selected text boxes—but you otherwise keep the appearance
of the text. For example, if you have threaded
three text boxes, the Remove Threading option
would unlink the three boxes, but all the text
would remain as-is. The other menu option is
Release Selection. This command removes a
selected text object from the thread. For example, if you had three boxes and selected the
middle one with the Selection tool (V), then you
chose Type>Threaded Text>Release Selection,
the text would flow from the first text box to
the third text box, skipping the middle box.

THREAD TEXT ON TWO PATHS

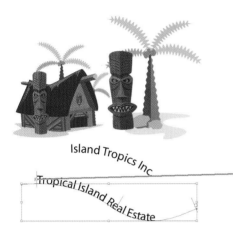

Hey, there's no rule that says you have to use closed shapes as text frames when you're threading text (mind you, in Illustrator 10 there was). You can also thread text on a path to another path, from a closed object to a path, or from a path to a closed object. Use the regular method of clicking on the first text object's Out Port icon (the tiny red box on the path with an plus sign [+] indicating text overflow), and then clicking on the next text object to create the thread.

TEXT WRAP AROUND A PHOTO

Any object in Illustrator can have text wrapped around it—any object created in Illustrator that is. Just position the object on top of a block of text using the Selection tool (V), and with the object still selected, go to the Object menu and choose Text Wrap>Make. If you want to have text wrap around an odd-shaped, placed raster image (File>Place), you'll have to create a path around the object. (In our example, we created and exported the path from Photoshop. See Chapter 11 for more details on exporting a path.) Then place your text box on top of the image and path, select just the path, and choose Object>Arrange>Bring to Front so the graphic is below the text and the path is above it. Then choose Object>Text Wrap>Make. In the Text Wrap Options dialog (Object>Text Wrap>Text Wrap Options), enter an Offset amount, and click OK. (*Note:* This won't work if your text and image are on different layers.)

MAKE A FRACTION

Another nice feature in Illustrator CS2 is support for OpenType fonts and their built-in special characters, including fractions. Choose an OpenType font by highlighting your text with the Type tool (T) and looking for the *O* symbol to the left of the font name in the Character palette's Font pop-up menu (in Windows, the symbol shows only in the Type>Font contextual menu). The symbol will only be visible if the Font Preview checkbox is turned on in Illustrator's Preferences dialog under Type.) Type the fraction you want as "x/x" (for example, 2/3 or 3/4), select the text, choose Type>OpenType from the Window menu and in the palette, click on the Fractions icon.

DON'T HAVE AN OPEN TYPE FONT?

But what if you need to make a fraction in a typeface that's not an Open-Type font? If you type "1/2" and go to the OpenType palette, the fraction button is grayed-out. Instead, click with the Type tool (T) where you want your fraction to appear but don't type anything, and then open the Glyphs palette (Window>Type>Glyphs).

Scroll through the palette to find the figure you need (in this example, a fraction) and double-click on it to add that character. Many fonts will offer the most-used fractions, such as 1/4, 1/2, and 3/4. (Seems obvious once you read it, doesn't it?) Needless to say, you can use this tip for any text symbols whose keyboard shortcut you can't remember, such as trademark, copyrights, accents, etc.

AUTOMATIC ORDINALS

What's an ordinal, you may ask? That's the official name for small, superscript text used after a numeral to denote a rank (e.g., 1st, 2nd, etc.). Rather than go to any trouble to create ordinals manually, some OpenType fonts have this function built right in. (OpenType fonts will have an *O* symbol next to the name in the Character palette's Font pop-up menu or the Type>Font contextual menu.) Just create some type using an OpenType font from the Character palette (found under Window>Type), select the text object with the Selection tool and in the OpenType palette (found under Window>Type), click on the Ordinals icon. The appropriate text will be converted into ordinals. Interestingly, any additional text you add to the existing type will also be converted into ordinals automatically. In our example, if we were to press the Return key (PC: Enter key) and type "5th" it would automatically change the "th" into an ordinal.

Awards

1st Place	Felix Nelson
2nd Place	Jim Gilbert
3rd Place	Brett Nyquist
4th Place	Freddie Maya

Awards

1st Place	Felix Nelson
2nd Place	Jim Gilbert
3rd Place	Brett Nyquist
4th Place	Freddie Maya

Character	Paragraph	OpenType
Figure:	Default Figure	
Position:	Default Position	

Ordinals

GLOBAL CHANGE CASE

The Change Case command (found under the Type menu) will change the case of highlighted type based on your choice in the Change Case submenu. (First, we chose UPPERCASE and then Sentence Case, in our examples.) You can also perform what you might call a "global" Change Case command by selecting multiple text objects with the Selection tool (V). Then when you use the Type>Change Case option, all text objects will change at once.

UPPERCASE   *Sentence Case*

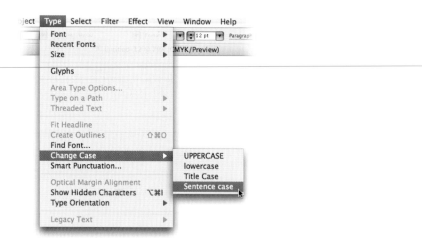

BLEND TWO TEXT OBJECTS

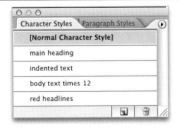

You can create some interesting effects by blending two text objects together, keeping the start and end text editable. Create two text objects that are not in text blocks by clicking once on the artboard with the Type tool (T), entering your text, and then clicking again in another location on the artboard, and creating a second text object. Select them both with the Selection tool and from the Object menu, choose Blend>Make, or press Command-Option-B (PC: Control-Alt-B). If you need to adjust the blend (such as change the number of steps), go back to the Object menu, and choose Blend>Blend Options.

YOUR STYLES IN EVERY DOCUMENT

Once you've created a series of character and paragraph styles, wouldn't it be nice to make them available in every new document you create? Well, if you read a couple of the other chapters, you can probably see where this is going. Save the document that contains your styles and then open the Adobe Illustrator Startup file (Illustrator CS2>Plug-ins folder). Go to the Window menu and choose Type>Character Styles. When the Character Styles palette opens, choose Load All Styles from the flyout menu. Navigate to the document you saved before, click Open, and all your styles should appear on the palette. Save the Startup file, restart Illustrator, and from then on your styles will be in every new document. (You'll have to do this in both the RGB and CMYK Startup files.)

Adobe Illustrator Startup_CMYK.ai @ 100% (CMYK/Preview)

Character Styles	Paragraph Styles
[Normal Character Style]	
main heading	
indented text	
body text times 12	
red headlines	

COLUMNS AND ROWS GALORE

Here's a simple way to create multiple columns (or rows) of text: Click-and-drag with the Type tool (T) to create a text block. Then, from the Type menu choose Area Type Options. Enter the number of columns (or rows) you want, the gutter width (space between columns), inset spacing you want, and click OK. Click in the text box, start typing, and the text will flow from one column (or row) to another within the text block.

COLUMNS AND ROWS IN ANY SHAPE

We'll admit it, once again this probably could have been part of the previous tip, but we thought we'd separate it, just in case you already knew the previous tip. This is the option to add rows and columns to more than just rectangles. Create any shape you want and then click near the shape's path with the Area Type tool (which is nested under the Type tool in the Toolbox). Then, while still using the Area Type tool, you can go to the Type menu and choose Area Type Options (as in the previous tip) to change the options for columns and rows.

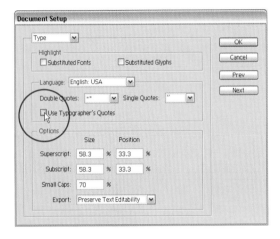

TURN OFF TYPOGRAPHER'S QUOTES

We almost hesitate to mention this one, because hopefully there aren't too many times where you'd want this option turned off. But, in case you don't want the quotation key to automatically turn into typographer's quotes (meaning you want straight quotes), you can turn off this option. From the File menu, choose Document Setup, select Type from the top pop-up menu, and uncheck Use Typographer's Quotes. Of course, if you change your mind, you can always convert "dumb" quotes back into "smart" quotes by selecting your text and choosing Type>Smart Punctuation. Make sure the Smart Quotes checkbox is turned on, and click OK.

PULL IT TOGETHER

5. Updates. If the Software is an upgrade or update to a previous version of the Software, you must possess a valid license to such previous version in order to use such upgrade or update. All upgrades and updates are provided to you on a license exchange basis. You agree that by using an upgrade or update you voluntarily terminate your right to use any previous version of the Software. As an exception, you may continue to use previous versions of the Software on your Computer after you use the upgrade or update but only to assist you in the transition to the upgrade or update, provided that the upgrade or update and the previous versions are installed on the same computer. Upgrades and updates may be licensed to you by Adobe with additional or different terms.

5. Updates. If the Software is an upgrade or update to a previous version of the Software, you must possessa valid license to such previous version in order to use such upgrade or update. All upgrades and updatesare provided to you on a license exchange basis. You agree that by using an upgrade or update youvoluntarily terminate your right to use any previous version of the Software. As an exception, you maycontinue to use previous versions of the Software on your Computer after you use the upgrade or updatebut only to assist you in the transition to the upgrade or update, provided that the upgrade or update and theprevious versions are installed on the same computer. Upgrades and updates may be licensed to you byAdobe with additional or different terms.

Sometimes when you open a PDF file in Illustrator, the text is editable but it comes in as a series of separate text blocks (or lines), instead of one big text block. Luckily, there's an easy fix. Use the Selection tool (V), with the Shift key held down, to select all the text blocks, then cut the text using the Command-X (PC: Control-X) keyboard shortcut. Drag out a text block with the Type tool (T) and press Command-V (PC: Control-V) to paste. Now the text will flow within one text block.

Friends

ILLUSTRATOR WITH

OTHER CS2 APPLICATIONS

By now you are probably either anti-cipating humorous chapter introductions, or skipping past them completely because you

Friends

illustrator with other CS2 applications

have realized they are pretty meaningless. Well, this one is different, and you should definitely read it. Why, you ask, is this intro more important than the others? Because it actually contains some pertinent information (surprise, surprise). Looking at other Illustrator CS2 books, we were surprised how little information there was about moving files between Illustrator and other applications. So, we have included a few tips that may seem like basic information (and frankly, they are). But we wanted to make sure you were not missing out just because everyone assumed that you knew this stuff already. So please bear with the basic tips that are mixed in with the more killer-esque tips. We now return to our regular chapter intro: "Two vector objects walk into a bar…"

EXPORT IN PHOTOSHOP FORMAT

To convert an Illustrator document into a Photoshop document complete with editable type layers, use the Export command from the File menu. Choose Photoshop (PSD file extension) from the Format pop-up menu at the bottom of the dialog and click Export (PC: Save). In the Photoshop Export Options dialog, choose the color model and resolution you need, but also make sure that the Write Layers radio button is selected, with Preserve Text Editability and Maximum Editability checked. (By the way, you may have read in some Illustrator CS2 books that you cannot export area type to Photoshop and preserve editability, but that's not true—you can.)

OPEN AN ILLUSTRATOR FILE IN PHOTOSHOP

To convert an Illustrator (.ai file extension) document into raster format, open it in Photoshop. In the dialog, enter the width, height, resolution, and mode for the raster version. Think carefully, because it is not easy to change your mind later without losing quality. If you're unsure, guess on the large side; you can always decrease the size or resolution later.

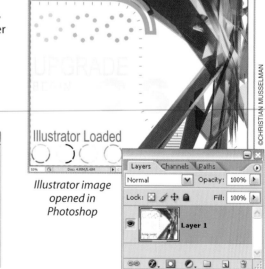

Illustrator image opened in Photoshop

PLACE AN .AI FILE INTO PHOTOSHOP

Add an Illustrator file into an open Photoshop document by choosing File>Place while in Photoshop. You won't get any options for mode or resolution, as those are set by the existing document. The only factor you can control is the physical size of the placed Illustrator file. After placing—and before the image is rasterized—the image has handles that let you resize it. Press-and-hold the Shift key to keep your image proportionate as you make the image larger or smaller. When you're finished resizing, press Return (PC: Enter) and the object will be rasterized at that size.

©MATT KLOSKOWSKI

DRAG-AND-DROP INTO PHOTOSHOP

Select an object in Illustrator with the Selection tool (V) and drag it into an open Photoshop document. Just as with placing an image, dragging-and-dropping an image results in handles for resizing the image. Is this method better than placing, or vice versa? It's really a matter of personal preference. Some people like to set up Illustrator and Photoshop side by side, and drag from one to the other, while others will prefer placing previously saved files. They both work well—it's really your choice.

DRAG-AND-DROP FROM DESKTOP

If you can see the photo you want to import into a document, rather than going to the File>
Place command, why not just drag it from the Desktop into the document? (Okay, so that was
the tip—drag-and-drop from the desktop to place a file into your existing document). The only
caveat is you will not get a dialog box with any options—the file will be linked. To embed the
file rather than link it, hold down the Shift key as you drag-and-drop the file.

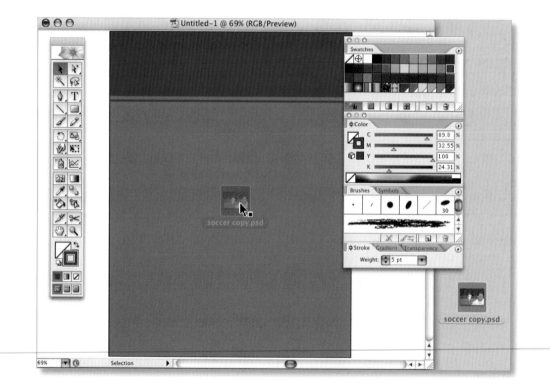

OPEN A PSD FILE IN ILLUSTRATOR

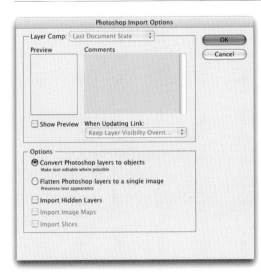

When you open a Photoshop (PSD) document in Illustrator, a dialog will offer two options: "Convert Photoshop layers to objects: Make text editable where possible," or "Flatten Photoshop layers to a single image: Preserves text appearance." Your choice depends on the level of editing you'd like to have. So, if you need to alter any layers in the Photoshop file, choose convert; if you don't need to alter the layered file, choose flatten.

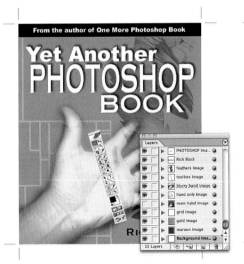

Converted PSD file

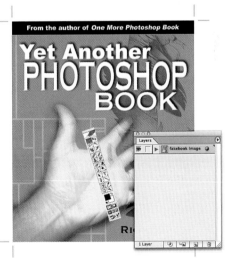

Flattened PSD file

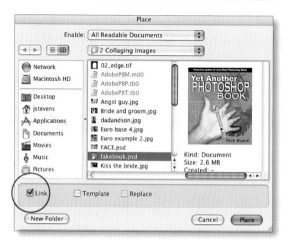

PLACE A PSD FILE INTO ILLUSTRATOR

Use the File>Place command to add a Photoshop document into an existing Illustrator document. In the Place dialog, you can choose to link the file or embed the image. To link the file, just choose the document you want to place and click on the Link checkbox at the bottom left of the dialog before you click the Place button. There actually isn't an option called "Embed," just don't select the Link checkbox in the Place dialog. A linked graphic is easier to edit in Photoshop, while an embedded PSD file makes your image more compatible with other applications.

To check if a file is linked or embedded, open the Links palette under the Window menu. An embedded graphic will have a small icon (aka: the Embedded Artwork icon) to the right of the image's name in the Links palette, while linked graphics do not have that icon. Want an even easier way? You can also click on the placed graphic with the Selection tool (V): A linked object has an X through it, while an embedded object does not.

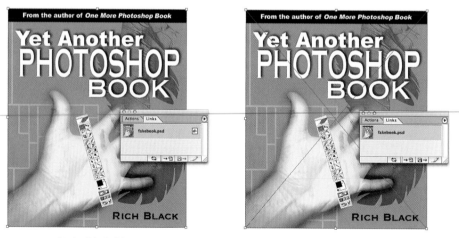

Embedded object   *Linked object*

PLACE IN ILLUSTRATOR FROM ADOBE BRIDGE

Check this out! You probably knew that you can open files directly from Adobe Bridge by double-clicking on them. If you have a PSD file, then double-clicking will launch the file in Photoshop. If you have an .ai or EPS file, then double-clicking it will launch that file in Illustrator. However, what if you want to open a Photoshop file in Illustrator or vice versa? You can place an image into Illustrator CS2 (or Photoshop, InDesign, or GoLive for that matter) right from within Bridge. Just choose File>Place and choose which application you'd like to place the file into.

CHANGE BETWEEN EMBEDDED AND LINKED GRAPHICS

It's easy to change a linked graphic to an embedded image. Open the Links palette under the Window menu, click on the linked graphic in the palette, and then from the palette's flyout menu, choose Embed Image. If the graphic has layers, you'll have to choose to either flatten it or convert it. It takes an extra step to change an embedded image into a linked image. After selecting the embedded graphic in the Links palette, choose Relink from the palette's flyout menu to open the Place dialog. Find your same graphic, turn on the Link checkbox, and click Place.

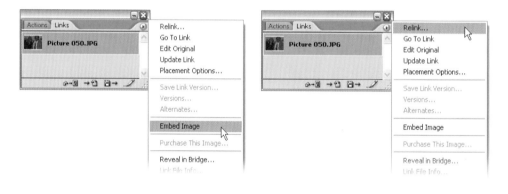

EDITING LINKED IMAGES

When you place an image into Illustrator, you have two options: embedding or linking. One of the advantages of linking an image is that you can edit it "on the fly" in the original software. Open the Links palette under the Window menu, and click on the Edit Original icon in the bottom-right corner of the palette. Or, to quickly edit the original without having to track down the Links palette, just hold down Command-Option (PC: Control-Alt) and double-click on the placed artwork. The appropriate software will automatically be launched and the image will be opened. Make your changes, save it, and the image will update in your Illustrator document. (You may get a warning dialog asking if you want to update linked files, depending on your preferences—see the tip on page 262.)

 **VECTOR SHAPES IN PHOTOSHOP**

When you export a document in PSD format, any vector shape is rasterized when it's opened in Photoshop. In order for an Illustrator vector shape to remain an editable vector—meaning you want to create a custom shape layer in Photoshop so you can edit the image—you must do one extra step in Illustrator before exporting. Select the object, choose Window>Pathfinder, and from the Pathfinder palette's flyout menu, choose Make Compound Shape. (*Note:* If your image has objects within it, just select its outermost bounding box. You don't need to flatten the image.) Then choose File>Export, and in the Format pop-up menu choose Photoshop (PSD). When you open the PSD file in Photoshop, the object will appear as a shape layer, preserving its vector editability.

Bull Dog Entertainment

Original vector image

Vector image in Photoshop

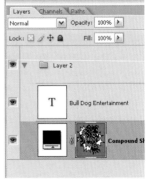

Rasterized vector image in Photoshop

Editable vector image in Photoshop

 **WITHOUT WARNING**

By default, every time you change and save a linked image in another application, you'll get a warning dialog asking you if you want to update the file in Illustrator. To avoid this warning every time you alter a linked image, press Command-K (PC: Control-K) to open the Preferences dialog and choose File Handling & Clipboard from the top-left pop-up menu. In the Update Links pop-up menu, choose Automatically. From then on, linked files will automatically update when you edit them in the original software, without any warning.

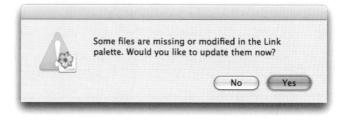

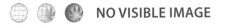 **NO VISIBLE IMAGE**

If you place a graphic (File>Place) and nothing shows up except an empty box, it probably means that the preview was turned off in the original program. You'll have to fix this problem by opening your image in its original editing software. In Photoshop, for example, there's an option that's set in the Preferences (Command-K [PC: Control-K]) under the File Handling category in the top-left pop-up menu in the dialog. In the Image Previews pop-up menu, choose Ask When Saving or Always Save. Then resave the image in Photoshop, and relink your selected image in Illustrator by choosing Relink in the Links palette's flyout menu.

 COPYING-AND-PASTING BETWEEN ILLUSTRATOR AND PHOTOSHOP

When you choose Copy from the Edit menu to copy a graphic in Illustrator and paste it into a Photoshop document (Edit>Paste), you get four choices: to paste as a Smart Object, as Pixels, as a Path, or as a Shape Layer. If you don't get this dialog offering these choices, you'll have to change a setting in Illustrator. Press Command-K (PC: Control-K) to go to Preferences, choose File Handling & Clipboard from the top-left pop-up menu in the dialog, and make sure that AICB (no transparency support) is checked. Copy the object again (Command-C [PC: Control-C]), and then switch to Photoshop and Paste (Command-V [PC: Control-V]). Now the Paste dialog will appear.

DRAG FROM ILLUSTRATOR TO MAKE A PATH IN PHOTOSHOP

If you know that you need a path in Photoshop, you can avoid the Paste dialog (see previous tip) by dragging-and-dropping an object from Illustrator into a Photoshop document. Just select your object with the Selection tool (V), hold down the Command key (PC: Control key) to override the Paste dialog, and drag-and-drop the object into your Photoshop document to automatically create a path. To ensure that your object was converted to a path in Photoshop, choose Paths from the Window menu. You should see a Work Path created in the palette for you. (In our example, the copied path was stroked with a brush in Photoshop after we selected Stroke Path from the Paths palette's flyout menu.)

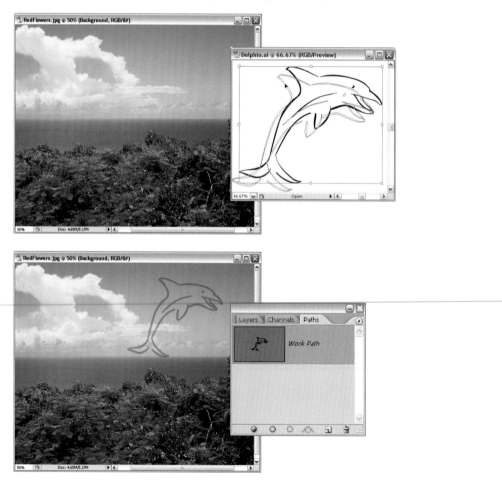

YOUR ILLUSTRATOR LOGO BUILT INTO PHOTOSHOP

If you would like your one-color logo to be a built-in part of Photoshop, accessible to every document, it's pretty simple to do. Keep in mind that this works best with basic compound shapes; so if you want to add effects, alter opacity, etc., you can simply do that in Photoshop. In Illustrator, select the logo with the Selection tool (V) (if the logo contains text, convert it to outlines by selecting the text with the Selection tool and choosing Type>Create Outlines) and then go to Edit>Copy (Command-C [PC: Control-C]). Switch to Photoshop, and from the Edit menu choose Paste (Command-V [PC: Control-V]). When the Paste dialog appears, choose Shape Layer (to access the Paste dialog, see the tip on page 263). When your logo appears in Photoshop, it will change to whatever fill or stroke color is active in Photoshop's Toolbox, but you can always change this later. So, with the logo still selected, go to the Edit menu and choose Define Custom Shape. Name it, click OK, and from then on your logo will appear in the Shape Picker when you have the Custom Shape tool (U) selected. Just choose a color in Photoshop's Toolbox, get the Custom Shape tool, choose your logo from the Shape Picker in the Options Bar, and click-and-drag with the Shift key held down to add your logo proportionately in any size you want!

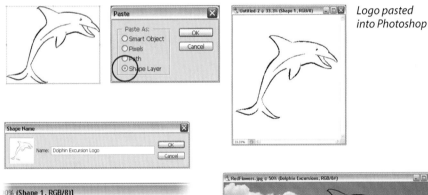

Logo pasted
into Photoshop

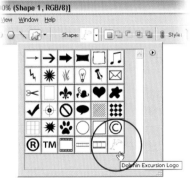

The dolphin logo in a Photoshop document

⊕ ⊕ ⊕ EXPORT PATHS FROM PHOTOSHOP

One very effective way to use Photoshop and Illustrator is to create a path in Photoshop (from a selection, for example), and use that path in Illustrator. To do this, go into Photoshop, open your document with your created path, and choose File>Export>Paths to Illustrator. In the resulting dialog, choose the appropriate path (which you saved when you created the path in Photoshop), in the Write pop-up menu, click OK, and open the resulting file in Illustrator. At first, you won't see anything except crop marks, which represent the boundaries of the Photoshop document. Switch to Outline mode from the View menu (Command-Y [PC: Control-Y]) to see, select, and start working with the path. (If you're unable to select or work with the path, you may need to use the Object>Expand command.)

⊕ ⊕ ⊕ BORROW SHAPES FROM PHOTOSHOP TO USE IN ILLUSTRATOR

Using this theory of exporting paths to Illustrator (see previous tip), why not take advantage of the many custom shapes that are built-in or can be loaded into Photoshop? Get the Custom Shape tool (U) and click the Paths icon in the Options Bar (it's the middle icon in the group of three icons on the left). Select an object from the Shape Picker in the Options Bar, then click-and-drag to create your object with the Custom Shape tool. This will create a Photoshop path. With the object still selected, choose File>Export>Paths to Illustrator to save the path. Now switch to Illustrator and go to File>Open to "transfer" the custom shape.

COMMON COLOR SETTINGS

Transparency Flattener Presets...
Tracing Presets...
Print Presets...
Adobe PDF Presets...

Color Settings...   Shift+Ctrl+K
Assign Profile...

Keyboard Shortcuts...   Alt+Shift+Ctrl+K
Preferences   ▶

When placing images created in Illustrator into Photo-shop (or vice versa), the colors may appear different. To fix this, ensure that the color management settings for both applications are the same. From Illustrator's Edit>Color Settings dialog, save your color management settings to a color settings file (CSF). From Photoshop's Edit>Color Settings dialog box, click the Load button, and load the CSF you just saved.

Color Settings

Unsynchronized: Your Creative Suite applications are not synchronized for consistent color. To synchronize, select Suite Color Settings in Bridge.

[OK]
[Cancel]
[Load...]
[Save...]

Settings: North America General Purpose 2

☐ Advanced Mode

Working Spaces
  RGB: sRGB IEC61966-2.1
  CMYK: U.S. Web Coated (SWOP) v2

Color Management Policies
  RGB: Preserve Embedded Profiles
  🔒 CMYK: Preserve Numbers (Ignore Linked Profiles)
  Profile Mismatches: ☐ Ask When Opening
                      ☐ Ask When Pasting
  Missing Profiles: ☐ Ask When Opening

Description:

TAKE YOUR SWATCHES ANYWHERE

Got a swatch set that you're using in Illustrator and want to use it in Photoshop or InDesign? Don't recreate all of the swatches all over again. Try using the new Save Swatches for Exchange function in the Swatches palette flyout menu (Window>Swatches). This will generate an ASE file that can be loaded into Photoshop CS2 and/or InDesign CS2, so you can take your swatches anywhere.

©MARK ANDERSON

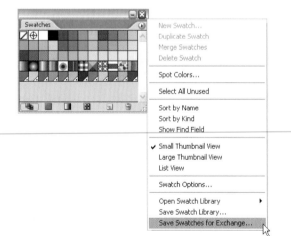

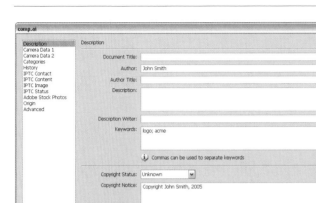

INFO FOR PHOTOSHOP

Embedding file info in Illustrator

The File Info command under the File menu is a very useful way to embed details about your document, including the author, keywords, and copyright information. As useful as it can be in Illustrator, the same information can be just as practical in Photoshop because that information becomes searchable metadata in Bridge. For instance, click on the Go to Bridge icon in the far right of Photoshop's Options Bar, navigate to find your Illustrator file, and click on the Metadata palette tab. Here you'll find all the file info that you embedded in your Illustrator document.

Embedded info visible in Bridge

METADATA TEMPLATES TO SAVE YOU TIME

If there is information that you need to include in multiple documents, you can make your life simpler by creating a metadata template. Use the File Info command under the File menu and enter the information you'd like to embed in your documents. Once you're done, use the flyout menu to choose Save Metadata Template. Anytime you need to embed the same information, go to File>File Info and use the flyout menu to choose from your saved templates. As an interesting aside, the same templates are available in Photoshop (and metadata templates created in Photoshop can be applied in Illustrator).

SHOW IMAGES OR PHOTOS IN OUTLINE MODE

By default, placed images are not visible in Outline mode (Command-Y [PC: Control-Y]). If you'd like to be able to see placed images while you're in Outline mode, go to Document Setup in the File menu. In the dialog that appears, check Show Images In Outline Mode. Any placed image will be visible, albeit in a poor-quality, black-and-white bitmapped version. Still, it can be helpful to see even this mediocre view if you're trying to edit objects in Outline mode.

©MATT KLOSKOWSKI

DASHED LINES IN PHOTOSHOP (THANKS TO ILLUSTRATOR)

The only way to create a dotted (or dashed) line in Photoshop is by playing with the Spacing slider in the Brushes palette found under the Window menu. It's a little clumsy, so why not take advantage of Illustrator's ability to create dashed lines? Draw a path with the Line tool (\). With the line selected, open the Stroke palette from the Window menu, choose Show Options from the palette's flyout menu, and turn on the Dashed Line checkbox to create a dashed line. Copy (Command-C [PC: Control-C]) the object in Illustrator, switch to your Photoshop document, and choose Paste (Command-V [PC: Control-V]). Voilà—a quick, dashed stroke! (In this example, we created a path in Photoshop, exported it to Illustrator choosing File>Export>Paths to Illustrator, added a dashed stroke, and pasted it back into Photoshop by choosing Paste in the Edit menu.)

STOP CLIPPING WHEN SAVING AS AN EPS

Sometimes when you save a document as an EPS file in Illustrator and place it into a page layout program, the EPS file appears to be "clipped"—missing some information at the edges. To make sure that doesn't happen, create a rectangle slightly larger than the artwork, with no fill or stroke. Then choose File>Save As, and in the dialog choose Illustrator EPS (EPS) in the Format (PC: Save as Type) pop-up menu. Clipping should no longer occur.

©JIB HUNT

ILLUSTRATOR LAYERS IN ACROBAT

One of the cool features in CS2 is the ability to take an Illustrator (.ai) file with multiple layers and save it as a PDF file, with those layers appearing in Acrobat. Yes, Acrobat 7.0 Professional (as well as Adobe Reader 7.0) has a Layers tab that works like a palette with the option to show and hide your Illustrator layers. Just choose File>Save As and in the dialog that appears, choose Adobe PDF (PDF) in the Format (PC: Save as Type) pop-up menu, then click Save. An Adobe PDF Options dialog will then appear, in which you change the Adobe PDF Preset pop-up menu to Custom, change the Compatibility pop-up menu to Acrobat 7 (PDF 1.6), and click the Create Acrobat Layers From Top-Level Layers checkbox. After you click Save PDF, open your document in Acrobat 7.0, and click the Layers tab on the left side of your document. Imagine having the ability to use Acrobat to show several versions of your document…

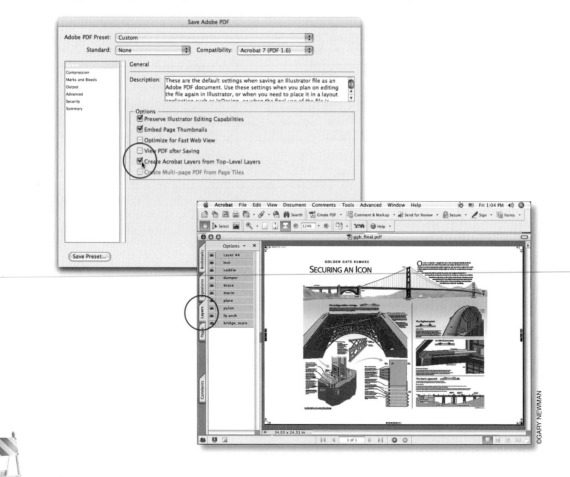

©GARY NEWMAN

OPEN A PDF IN ILLUSTRATOR

Besides Acrobat, Illustrator is one of the few software programs that can open and edit PDF files. Go to File>Open and target the PDF file. If it is a multipage document, a dialog will appear that allows you to navigate to the single page you'd like to open. (Unfortunately, you'll have to base that decision on a pretty small preview window.) If you open a page, edit it, and choose Save in the File menu, it will be saved back as part of the multipage document. To separate the image from the multipage document—converting it into a one-page PDF file—choose Save As from the File menu, rename the file, and click Save.

PLACE A PDF WITH SPOT COLOR

If you create a spot-color document in Photoshop (that is, with one or more spot color channels) and place it into Illustrator (File>Place), you probably want the spot color to preview. Unfortunately, if you save the file as an EPS file in Photoshop (File>Save As and choose Photoshop EPS in the Format [PC: Save as Type] pop-up menu), and place it into Illustrator, the spot color will import with the EPS file, but it will not show in the placed file. Instead, in Photoshop choose Save As from the File menu and select Photoshop PDF in the Format (PC: Save as Type) pop-up menu (making sure you have the Spot Colors checkbox selected). Switch to your Illustrator document and choose File>Place. When your image appears, go to the View menu and choose Overprint Preview (Command-Option-Shift-Y [PC: Control-Alt-Shift-Y]).

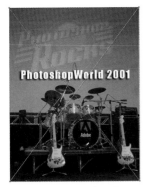

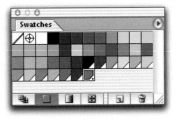

Document placed as Photoshop EPS

Document placed as Photoshop PDF

SENDING A FILE TO A SERVICE BUREAU

Before you create a document that will be printed at an outside service provider (such as a large format printer), see if you can get a copy of the bureau's printer driver. Load it on your system and choose it in the Print dialog (File>Print). That way, you can make sure all the settings are correct and that your document is set up correctly before sending it off to print.

Fiery 2345XT

REDUCE FILE SIZE

Before saving a file, you can cut down the file size by removing all unnecessary stuff in the file (in this instance, stuff meaning swatches, symbols, patterns, etc.). Thanks to Adobe, it's pretty easy. In the Actions palette (Window>Actions), look in the Default Actions folder for Delete Unused Palette Items. Click on the action name, and press the Play Current Selection button at the bottom of the palette to run the action. All the unused stuff will be removed, so that when you save the document, it will be a little smaller (not all that much in some cases, but every little bit helps, right?).

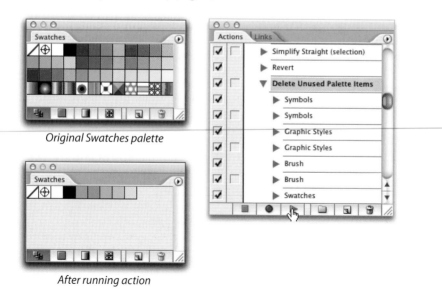

Original Swatches palette

After running action

CLEANING UP YOUR ILLUSTRATIONS

Before printing a file, you can do yourself a favor by "cleaning it up." First, from the Object menu choose Path>Clean Up. In the dialog, make sure you select the Stray Points and Empty Text Paths checkboxes. Click OK to delete all these unneeded points. If you're sending the document to an outside printing service, you may also want to go to the Swatches palette and use the pop-up menu to choose Select All Unused. Then click on the Trash icon at the bottom of the palette to delete the swatches. Save the document (File>Save), and you're ready to go.

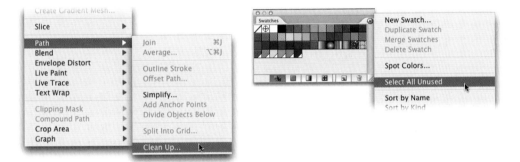

SAVE FOR OLDER VERSIONS OF ILLUSTRATOR

Illustrator is not backwards compatible, which means that you cannot save an Illustrator CS2 file into an older version such as 10, 9, or earlier. The best way to create a document that can be read by an older version of Illustrator is to choose the Save As command in the File menu (Command-Shift-S [PC: Control-Shift-S]). Click Save and from the Illustrator Options dialog, you can choose from older versions of the program in the Version pop-up menu. Be aware that several functions—notably type—will not transfer well from CS2 into earlier versions. (*Note:* If you attempt to open an Illustrator CS2 file in Illustrator 10, you'll get a dialog saying that the file was created in a newer version of Illustrator, but it does give you the option to import the file. Opening a file in this manner does not maintain the CS2 formatting as well as using the Export option.)

 **TRIAL SEPARATION**

Before sending your file off to the service bureau for color separations, you can (and probably should) print a test separation on your own printer. Use the Print command from the File
menu (Command-P [PC: Control-P]) and click on the Output category on the left-hand side
of the dialog. Under the Output option, change the Mode pop-up menu from Composite to
Separations (Host-Based). That way you can make sure that only the appropriate number of
colors print.

 **PRINTING EVEN LARGER THAN ILLUSTRATOR WILL LET YOU**

Adobe Illustrator

⚠ The value must be between 0.0139 in and 227.5416 in.

[OK]

If you haven't figured this out yet, the largest document Illustrator will let you create is 227.54 inches in width or height. How do I know this? Try creating a new document that is 250 inches in size and Illustrator will give you a little reminder of the maximum settings.

Well, what if you need to print something out that is larger than this? There's a way to cheat a little and it's in the Print dialog box (Command-P [PC: Control-P]). Under Options, near the bottom of the dialog, just click Custom Scale and enter in a percentage scale value that will get you to the print size you need. For example, if you need to print something that is 260 inches in width and height, then create a document that is 200 inches instead. Then enter 130% in the Width and Height settings under Custom Scale. This will print out at 260 inches (200 * 1.30 = 260).

Print

Print Preset: Custom ▾

Printer: Tektronix Phaser 850DX ▾

PPD: Default (Tektronix Phaser 850DX) ▾

General
Setup
Marks and Bleed
Output
Graphics
Color Management
Advanced
Summary

General

Copies: 1 ☐ Collate ☐ Reverse Order

Pages: ⦿ All
⦿ Range:
☐ Skip Blank Pages

Media
Size: Defined by Driver ▾

Width: 612 pt   Height: 792 pt

Orientation: ▢ ▢ ▢ ▢ ☐ Transverse

Options
Print Layers: Visible & Printable Layers ▾
◯ Do Not Scale
◯ Fit to Page
⦿ Custom Scale: Width: 130 ▨ Height: 130

©MATT KLOSKOWSKI

[Save Preset...] [Setup...]   [Print] [Cancel] [Done]

 **SAVE PRESET FOR PRINTING**

If you have more than one printer in your location, or you send out files to various print shops, you can easily create printer presets for these different locations. Just set up the options in the Print dialog (File>Print) as if you were going to print to one of your printers (or as if you were setting up the file to send to the print shop). Rather than printing, though, click the Save Preset button, name the preset, and then click Done (instead of the Print button). Now, anytime you use the Print command from the File menu, you can choose from a list of presets in the Print Preset pop-up menu in the Print dialog. This can be a great timesaver, avoiding the need to change settings every time you change printers.

SAVING PRINT SETTINGS

In addition to saving presets (as mentioned in the previous tip), if you need to change the page setup and other settings for a document—without printing—you can do this in the Print dialog. Go to File>Print and just change the settings, such as page setup options, printer marks, etc., and then click the Done button rather than Print. Your settings will reappear when you reopen the Print dialog.

SAVE FOR WEB RIGHT WITHIN ILLUSTRATOR

Many people don't realize that in the File menu, Illustrator has a similar Save for Web interface as Photoshop. This is especially useful if you're saving Web graphic icons, as the PNG format is popular for this type of work. Illustrator's Save for Web dialog even includes a 2- and 4-up view, which really helps get a preview of how your vector artwork will look when compressed using various Web image compression formats.

START OVER IN SAVE FOR WEB

Often, when you're using the Save for Web command in the File menu, you'll find yourself experimenting with various settings. Should you ever want to start again from square one, you can reset all settings in the dialog by holding down the Option key (PC: Alt key). When you do this, the Cancel button changes to Reset. Click Reset to put all settings back to their defaults.

REMEMBER YOUR SAVE FOR WEB SETTINGS

Here's a cool way to remember a setting and then experiment further, knowing you can revert to these settings. To do this, go to the File menu, choose Save for Web, and then choose your settings. When you're finished, hold down the Option key (PC: Alt key) to change the Done button to Remember. Now you can feel free to experiment, knowing that you can go back to this remembered setting by clicking the Reset button. (As mentioned in the previous tip, hold down the Option key [PC: Alt key] to change the Cancel button to Reset.)

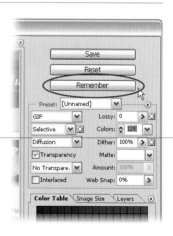

OPTIMIZE BY FILE SIZE

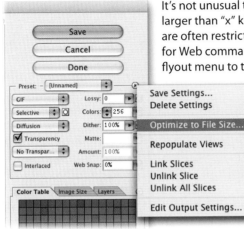

It's not unusual to get a request for a Web graphic to be no larger than "x" kilobytes. Advertising banners, for example, are often restricted to a maximum file size. Luckily, the Save for Web command in the File menu can help with that; in the flyout menu to the right of the preset options in the Save for Web dialog, choose Optimize to File Size. Enter the size for your graphic, click OK, and Save for Web will do the rest.

FLATTENER PREVIEW

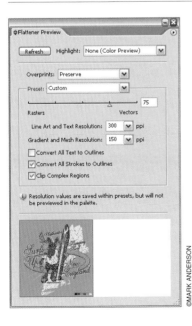

©MARK ANDERSON

Before sending files off to print, you may need to use the Flatten Transparency command in the Object menu. Unfortunately, the preview function in this dialog can take a while, so here's an alternative: From the Window menu, choose the Flattener Preview palette, then in the palette's flyout menu choose Show Options. There you can get a much quicker preview of the areas that would be affected by flattening, when you select Quick Preview from the palette's flyout menu. To see the preview, be sure to click the Refresh button at the top of the palette. (*Note:* Resolution values cannot be previewed in the palette.)

GET YOUR GRADIENTS TO PRINT

If you're having trouble getting gradients and gradient meshes to print properly, there is one setting you can change. But be warned, only change this if you're unable to get gradients to print properly, because if you leave this option on, printing can become extremely slow. Open the Print dialog from the File menu, click on the Graphics category in the left-hand side of the dialog, then turn on the checkbox beside Compatible Gradient and Gradient Mesh Printing. (*Note:* You'll likely get a warning dialog informing you that this option should be selected *only* if you're having problems printing.) The current raster resolution will be shown just below the checkbox, and if it's set too low, you'll have to click the Cancel button and use the Document Raster Effects Settings under the Effect menu to change the resolution. If you read the previous chapters, you know that changing raster effects settings after you've applied filters and effects can alter these effects, so remember—only use this if you're unable to print gradients on your printer (this is common in older printers).

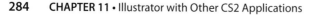

©JOHN SCHWEGEL

MISS THE OLD GAL?

Okay, so this really has nothing to do with this chapter, but I thought I'd sneak it in here… just because. For all of its life, Illustrator has always used Botticelli's Venus as its symbol. Then in the CS and CS2 versions, she went away, replaced by flowers. If you miss the old look, you can get a glimpse of the past by holding down the Option key (PC: Alt key) and choosing About Illustrator. In OS X on the Mac, it's under the Illustrator menu; in Windows XP, it's under the Help menu.

Adobe® **Illustrator**®CS2

12.0.0

Created by the Adobe Illustrator Team.

Legal Notices   Credits

Matt
KW Media
Adobe   11311296 153595760429

Adobe® **Illustrator**®CS2

12.0.0

Created by the Adobe Illustrator Team.

Legal Notices   Credits

Matt
KW Media
Adobe   11311296 153595760429

Index

D

dashed lines, converting to outline, 114
Data command (Object menu), 64
data graphs, 64
defaults
  colors, fill and stroke, 17
  fonts, 212
  measurement override, 39
  workspaces, 30
Deselect command (Select menu), 13
Design command (Object menu), 66
designs, graphs, 66
Desktop, drag-and-drop from, 256
dialogs
  3D Options, 196
  3D Revolve Options, 199
  Art Brush Options, 41
  Blend Options, 70, 73
  Calligraphic Brush Options, 5, 206
  Color Settings, 267
  Expand, 77
  Flatten Transparency, 114
  Graph Design, 66
  Graph Type, 65
  Insert Menu Item, 52
  Keyboard Shortcuts, 25
  Layers Options, 156
  Levels, 75
  Move, quick access, 10
  Palette Options, 52, 165
  Photoshop Export Options, 254
  PNG Options, 24
  Preferences, 43
  Save for Web, 283
  Scale, 106
  Scatter Brush Options, 201
  scrubby sliders, 181
  Text Import Options, 19
  Transform Effect, 102
DIM images, layers, 156
Direct Selection tool, 8, 9, 60, 67
Distort & Transform command (Effect menu), 18, 102
Distort command (Filter menu), 18
Divide Objects Below command (Object menu), 78
Document Info command (Window menu), 44
Document Info palette, 44
documents
  automatically adding rulers, 37
  creating multiple pages, 56–57
duplicating settings, 54
  information, 44
  raster settings, 188
Don't Show Center icon, 43
downloads
  Adobe Studio Exchange website, 53
  free symbols, 205
  presets, 4
drag-and-drop objects, 115
drag-and-drop text, 232
drop shadows, 187
Dry Brush command (Effect menu), 186

E

Edit menu commands
  Color Settings, 267
  Copy, 95
  Keyboard Shortcuts, 25
  Paste, 95
Effect Gallery command (Effect menu), 180
Effect menu commands
  3D, 80
  Artistic, 186
  Brush Strokes, 189
  Convert to Shape, 69
  Distort & Transform, 18, 102
  Effect Gallery, 180
  Stylize, 229
  Transform, 102
effects. See also appearances; styles
  3D objects, 80
    artwork, 199
      banner creation, 197
      rotating, 196
  apply same again, 185
  drop shadows, 187
  gallery, 180
  grayed out, 195
  permanent, 63
  pop art dot, 184
  raster settings, 188
  reset settings, 186
  scaling, 106
  switching between RGB and CMYK, 189
  Symbol Stainer tool, 201–202
  three dimensional, view while applying, 195
  versus filters, 18, 185
  vintage texture, 89
embedded objects, 258, 260

Envelope Distort command (Object menu), 114, 238
EPS file, clipping, 273
Expand command (Object menu), 19, 77, 136
Expand dialog, 77
expanded palettes, 7
Export command (File menu), 24, 254
exporting
  Photoshop format, 254
  preview image turned on, 263
Extrude & Bevel command (Effects menu), 80, 197
Eyedropper tool, 119, 123, 128, 182

F

fading colors, 137
feedback, 6
Ferris, Todd, 146
fields, palettes, 54
File Handling & Clipboard command, 262
File Info command (File menu), 269
File menu commands
  Export, 24, 254
  File Info, 269
  New From Template, 22
  Place, 19, 60, 156
  Print, 56
  Save As Template, 23
  Save for Web, 282
files
  clean up, 277
  reducing size, 276
  saving for older Illustrator versions, 277
Fill Color command (Select menu), 99
Fill icon, 17
fills
  colors, 130
  default colors, 17
  effecting, 21
  none, 130
  swapping to opposite, 131
Filter menu commands
  Colors, 134
  Distort, 18
  Stylize, 181
filters
  grayed out, 195
  reset settings, 186
  versus effects, 18, 185

COLOPHON

The book was produced by the authors and design team using all Macintosh computers, including a Power Mac G5 1.8-GHz, a Power Mac G5 Dual Processor 1.8-GHz, a Power Mac G5 Dual Processor 2-GHz, a Power Mac G4 Dual Processor 1.25-MHz. We use LaCie, Sony, and Apple Studio Display monitors.

Page layout was done using Adobe InDesign CS. We use a Mac OS X server, and burn our CDs to our CPU's internal Sony DVD RW DW-U10A.

The headers for each technique are set in Adobe Myriad Pro Semibold at 11 points on 12.5 leading, with the Horizontal Scaling set to 100%. Body copy is set using Adobe Myriad Pro Regular at 9.5 points on 11.5 leading, with the Horizontal Scaling set to 100%.

Screen captures were made with Snapz Pro X and were placed and sized within Adobe InDesign CS. The book was output at 150 line screen, and all in-house printing was done using a Tektronix Phaser 7700 by Xerox.

ADDITIONAL RESOURCES

Layers Magazine
Layers—The How-To Magazine for Everything Adobe—is the foremost authority on Adobe's design, digital video, digital photography, and education applications. Each issue features timely product news, plus the quick tips, hidden shortcuts, and step-by-step tutorials for working in today's digital market.

http://www.layersmagazine.com

KW Computer Training Videos
Dave Cross and Matt Kloskowski are featured in a series of Photoshop and Photoshop Elements training DVDs, available from KW Computer Training. Visit the website or call 813-433-5000 for orders or more information.

http://www.photoshopvideos.com

National Association of Photoshop Professionals (NAPP)
The industry trade association for Adobe® Photoshop® users and the world's leading resource for Photoshop training, education, and news.

http://www.photoshopuser.com

Adobe Photoshop Seminar Tour
See Dave Cross live at the Adobe Photoshop Seminar Tour, the nation's most popular Photoshop seminars. For upcoming tour dates and class schedules, visit the tour website.

http://www.photoshopseminars.com

Photoshop World Conference & Expo
The convention for Adobe Photoshop users has now become the largest Photoshop-only event in the world.

http://www.photoshopworld.com

You've got the people. You've got the projects. You've got the ideas.

(Do you have the technology to bring them together?)

When creativity is your business, you need technology that doesn't get in the way of your ideas. That's why CDW carries all of the technology products a creative professional needs from the brands you trust like Adobe, Epson, Canon, Extensis, Pantone and more. Our account managers will also get you quick answers to your questions. And with fast shipping and access to the industry's largest inventories, you'll get the products you need, when you need them. So give us a call and find out how we make it happen. Every order, every call, every time.

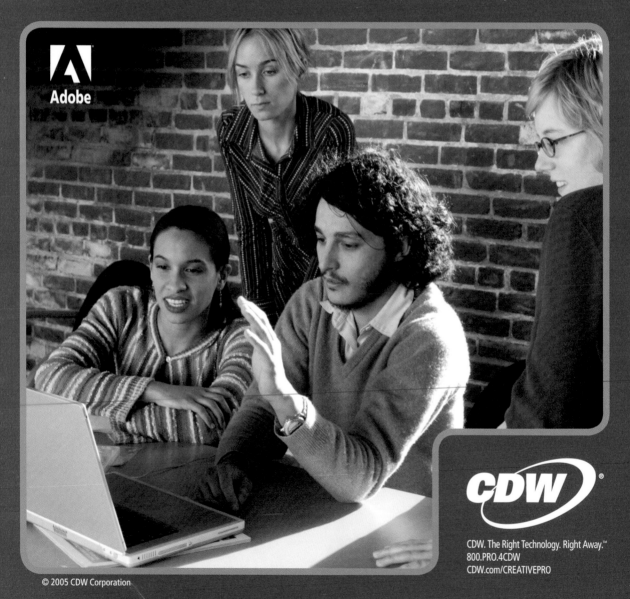

Adobe

CDW. The Right Technology. Right Away.™
800.PRO.4CDW
CDW.com/CREATIVEPRO